A VOYAGE WITH GOD

SOUNDING THE CALL FOR UNITY AND DECLARING WAR ON THE DARKNESS

PHILLIP BLAIR

A Voyage with God: Sounding the Call for Unity and Declaring War on the Darkness

Copyright © 2008 Phillip Blair

Written by: Phillip Blair

Author Photo by: Phillip Blair

Book Cover Design by: Donald Semora

This book is the work of solely the author. All incidents and dialogue, and all characters with the exception of certain well known historical and public places and figures, are the products of the author's own personal religious convictions, opinions, and ideas, and are not the ideas or opinions of the publisher. In all other respects and situations in the book, any resemblance to any persons alive or dead is purely coincidental unless specifically noted.

ISBN Number: 978-1-511675-50-5

10 9 8 7 6 5 4 3 2 1

All Rights Reserved. This book may not be copied, reproduced, transmitted or stored by any means, including graphic, electronic or mechanical without the express written consent of the author except in cases of brief quotations, critical reviews, and certain other noncommercial uses permitted by copyright law.

Printed and Published in the United States of America

This book is dedicated to my Father in Heaven. Thank you for choosing me for this task and for never giving up on me, even when I had given up on myself. Also to my children, Jackson and Jeremiah.

"A voice cries: 'In the wilderness prepare the way of the Lord; make straight in the desert a highway for our God. Every valley shall be lifted up, and every mountain and hill made low; the uneven ground shall become level, and the rough places a plain. And the glory of the Lord shall be revealed, and all flesh shall see it together, for the mouth of the Lord has spoken.'"

(Isaiah 40:3-5 ESV)

Heed the Call!

26 He will raise a signal for nations far away,
and whistle for them from the ends of the earth;
and behold, quickly, speedily they come!
27 None is weary, none stumbles,
none slumbers or sleeps,
not a waistband is loose,
not a sandal strap broken;
28 their arrows are sharp,
all their bows bent,
their horses' hoofs seem like flint,
and their wheels like the whirlwind.
29 Their roaring is like a lion,
like young lions they roar;
they growl and seize their prey;
they carry it off, and none can rescue.
30 They will growl over it on that day,
like the growling of the sea.
And if one looks to the land,
behold, darkness and distress;
and the light is darkened by its clouds.

```
Isaiah 5:26-30, ESV
```

TABLE OF CONTENTS

INTRODUCTION	11
PART ONE	15
RENDER YOUR HEART	17
PURPOSE WITH GOD	18
GOD'S EYES	19
A STORM SO CALM	22
STAR LIGHT	27
AS THE CLOUDS PASS BY	30
DEEP INSIDE	36
STRENGTH FROM THE SUN	41
A BREATH OF LIFE	47
POWER AND PRAISE	51
VIVID SCENES	57
PART TWO	65
HOLY DIVINE	67

SUNSHINE IN THE RAIN	72
GLORIOUS PRESENCE	78
PRECIOUS GEMS	86
WORD OF GOD	93
SIGNS OF THE TIMES	101
THE END	106
JUDGMENT	113
PART THREE	119
CALL TO BATTLE	121
CALL TO REPENTANCE	130
WORTHY OF THE BATTLE	143
VICTORY IN OUR LORD JESUS	155
SOUNDING THE BATTLE CRY	162
THE GUIDING HOPE OF GLORIOUS DESTINY	177
FINAL WORDS	180
THE LION WILL OVERCOME!	185

Introduction

In every Christian's life, there is that moment when God calls you. Oftentimes it doesn't come right away, and each calling is vastly different, but when you seek the face of God, He reveals His plans to His children.

My calling was made known to me at 15 years old, shortly after being saved. It was loud and it was scary. I sought the face of God with zeal and determination. During this time, I wrote the words of this book. After almost a year, I walked away from God altogether. I knew He was still there, and He tried several times to call me back, but I turned bitter and made mistakes. Fast forward 14 years and I have made more mistakes than I can count, but He has remained faithful.

When writing *A Voyage with God* in 2001, the book began with a vision where I was sitting in a boat, or vessel as the book refers to it, and surrounding me as far as the eye can see is the ocean. Along the vast horizon, I see a strength which calls me to come near. I know in my heart my duty, and I begin to write.

Read *A Voyage with God* as if you are that young Christian beginning your relationship with God and let yourself grow with the book. Allow God to speak to you through the words and let your purpose become known. If you know your purpose, allow Him to reaffirm or confirm your calling and step forward to be used. Line up in rank and file, and let's go to work bringing the gospel to a world that has forsaken their God. There are billions of people who do not know Jesus and follow another God.

We must change this fact and bring the real truth, the gospel of Jesus Christ, to the ends of the earth.

Now is the time. The urgency is on the wind and the storm is coming. There is no more time to delay or tarry in the ways of this world. Mount up as a soldier of God and let's go to work. Make disciples and tell them to follow you as you follow Jesus. Jesus taught this (Matthew 28:19) and Paul was great at following God's command (see Acts). Be obedient and faithful to His words.

Open your heart and mind for the bold claims in this book. Allow the Holy Spirit to work in you and test the spirits (1 John 4:1), as you should. There have come into this world many false prophets and many more shall rise up claiming prosperity and peace. These are not of the Lord. Be vigilant and diligent in your walk and seek out his ways in all things (Isaiah 55:8).

Read with the Holy Spirit guiding you and ask the Lord to reveal His plan for your life. There are many words in this book encoded for specifically chosen soldiers of God. I write in obedience and admittedly there are many ideas and revelations in this book I do not truly understand. Ask our God for clarity, purpose, and direction. There is much fulfillment to be had from these promises. Seek the face of God, and His plan will come alive to His children.

Read with eager anticipation of the future of the world, for though gray turns to black and the night will become darker than ever before, there is so much hope. The Spirit of God shall be restored, and people will forsake the ways of the world to once again follow Him. Take heed, however, for the darkness shall rise against you. Prepare yourselves in mind and spirit for the coming times. This book hopes to help in that regard. Enjoy!

PART ONE
PURPOSE and DIRECTION

Render Your Heart

My Commission

"Bow breaks into the open air. Across the vivid sky flash scenes of the upcoming era. Producing light of a new day, your life flashes by in an instant, and you long for the burdens to go away. As the air caresses your face, you smile and know that love was brought with them, and your understanding will blossom with the flowers. Knowing and seeing all around you—that life was brought with a purpose—you release your guilt and in time you will progress into the eyes of a new being. Undoubtedly, this day will bring new hope to people's lives and relinquish their own worries. Time progresses and no rush will life cause. Patience, the key to understanding, is in your hands. Grasp it, and take heed to the before and after. Release your worries. Live day by day in sight of what is to come. Your eyes are filled with the benevolence of a worthy justice. Render your heart and speak truth in the eyes of your transgressors. Let it be known and speak pure the words of the Almighty God. Test their ways. Leave them tainted for judgment will come. But let your voice be heard through the thousands. Erase your faults and believe My words. Remember the day and vow on its word that no more will this go by without judgment. Release your pride and exalt your Lord. Lead the life I have made for you. Uphold the responsibility of your duties. You are my child, and I love you. Rejoice and let it be known."

Purpose with God

Along the vast horizon of never-ending joy, I see a strength which carries its own light. Surrounded by the ocean whose waves caress the Earth, I sit and observe the fullness of its greatness. Allowing only few, I know this strength is connected with my heart. I sit and stare out at the endless ocean only to see a compelling light that hovers. It swiftly soars to and fro across the waters motioning me to come near. I sit in awe, unaware of anything else. I try to understand the concern of the strength which holds me. It cries out at me, motioning for my help. I undoubtedly hold the key to this phenomenon and unaware of what it might be I become frustrated.

Ever so gently, I drift along the now still waters across this endless ocean, warily waiting on the strength to show meaning in my eyes. Patiently, I sit longing for an answer. This strength, able to hold the sun at its place and shatter the world in its fingertips, sits waiting for me to answer its plea. Too far to hear the words, I weep for I'm now emotionally involved. Only the cry must be heard. Unable to do anything but sit and watch this beautiful array of light, I look for a sign to help me understand the problem which has been aroused. Soaring over water, the compelling light connects with my heart, and I understand the fullness of the situation presented before me.

Bewildered, I wonder what I'm involved for. Visions surround me and my intentions are understood. The strength which sits vaguely but distinguishable along the horizon now portrays the outline of a human. Above the human sits a rainbow with a heart inscribed within it. Never-ending hope for all of the human race—those made with His love—is the compelling light. It shows that one day hope will be all that's left. The one thing created in life and filled with love now hates its Maker. It curses His name and ignores His cries.

The drift is time. Time moves ever so slowly in a never-ending flow. But one day the light from the strength will reach out and grab you, bringing you home. The outline of the human means we were created in His image, by His love, and He will have mercy on us. But time is running short. Mercy is only temporary. Our constant drift will carry us either way.

Arrays of light dance across the vivid sky, and I weep with joy. I raise my sails for the winds pick up and purposely move towards the strength which holds my heart. The aspects of my life are understood, and yet my duties are unfulfilled.

God's Eyes

Solemn and holy, I drift forward into the pedestal of time. It is where the quiet hours of the morning shine brightest and full of life. Light beams from a dawn of new earthly days of heavenly giving and praise. Cheerfully, we announce the glory of the One behind it all. Translucent as the water's edge and given in glory to God, holy and righteous are those eyes of the bright blue waves. Faithful and wondrous are the ways of God, for I drift along the wake of God's plan and realize all of the blessings provided along the route.

Without worry or distress, the eyes of God see me through each day. Those peaceful eyes lead me ahead into a new dawn of endless possibility and the beginning of an era beyond any of humankind's comprehension. I long for the boundless glories of Heaven to shine peace upon the world and to pour from the sky, but inside I know time will heal the hurt of an ungodly world, the majesty of God shall one day be shown, and I will forever dwell in the house of my Lord God Almighty.

I raise my hands to God and praise His holy name, for He alone is the author and finisher of my faith. I gaze at the vast surroundings of my newfound habitat and realize that all will be justified when the time is right. I search the sky, and the wondrous presence of God manifests. The power of God surrounds me and so I gasp for air and fall on my face as though dead. No feeling of life but the rock and tumble of the ocean's waves around me, my spirit rises with the tugging breeze of God's Spirit and unites me as one with the wind while I sing the tune of His Holy Majesty. My life and body, dead and without value, realizes that through the strength of God, I can do all things (Philippians 4:13). I am everything, because He is everything inside of me. His Spirit guides me, and I supplicate in all situations with praise and thanksgiving (Philippians 4:6), through trial and tribulation. For I know the sufferings of this present time are nothing to be compared with the glory that shall be revealed to us in Christ Jesus (Romans 8:18), for my God will supply every need according to His riches and glory

(Philippians 4:19). Without God, I am nothing and have nothing. With Him, I can move mountains (Mark 11:23).

Casting off my mortal flesh, my Spirit lives forever in the promises of my Lord Jesus, for He proclaims: **"I am the God of Abraham, and the God of Isaac, and the God of Jacob,"** and **"He is not God of the dead, but of the living"** (Matthew 22:32). With this promise, I have been set free from the bondages of sin and death (Romans 8:2) and released unto the world as an instrument of God to fulfill His will in this time and purpose. There is no other choice. The mission is at hand, and the calling must be fulfilled, for **"many are called, but few are chosen"** (Matthew 22:14).

Heavenly harkening to the Son of Man without flaw and on wondrous occasion, my spirit reunites with lifeless bone and marrow and the fleshly body which eagerly awaits. Now righteous and holy by the blood of Jesus, my body speaks true the word of the Almighty God and proclaims in all His power and glory the work of Christ Jesus. Separated from the world, I voyage on in pursuit of closeness and fulfillment of His will. Only by faith will I succeed in this newfound voyage, and one day I will return to my master having accomplished His purpose through obedience and great sacrifice.

I stand upon the bow of discovery and look at God's wondrous eyes once more. His tearful gifts are poured abundantly upon me with a hope of shedding new peace and understanding amidst a world of bitter deceit. I give joyful thanks to the God of all creation and hope the wake from my own life and vessel will lead all others of faith to the restful arms of our Lord. I journey on in reflection of the past but rejoice with the thought of coming days and all it will bring. The intentions of my life are understood, and yet my duties remain unfulfilled.

A Storm So Calm

Sailing on in this voyage of everlasting peace, I search the sky and find it full of wondrous blessings from the Father. I long for the day to come when I shall stand in His holy presence and proclaim the power of my Almighty Savior. However, a violent and unrelenting storm approaches from across the vastness of the sky and is headed our way. I cry out to God and ask Him for His help in making it through the coming temptations and for Him to guide me through this malignancy. Terror stricken and emotional, I weep for the storm is ever so violent, and the other ships would not hold course without proper warning of what is to come. I sit and begin to write, knowing the storm will pass me by without doing any harm. But the time draws near to the coming of the Son of Man.

The certainties of my duties surround me, and I know it is one of shedding a light of truth into the darkness, for the completion of the will of God only comes by the hands of those believers willing to be used. This is a clarion call to gather the troops throughout the earth, for they are weary and scattered, but the strength of the Lord shall bind us together for the coming times! Let us go before the Lord in Spirit and in truth for our days are numbered. The declaration from the horn of God shall soon be sounded. The lights shall fade in the midst of the weary, and the horn of the broken shall be raised up from ashes in the truth.

There is only one storm, and there is only one chance left. Be raised up or be forgotten in a sick and sinful land. There is no more delay. The time is now, and the sands upon the shore are limitless in comparison to what God shall do through you and with the name of Jesus Christ upon your lips.

"Do you not know the plans I have for you?" says the Lord. **"Listen to Me, and I will give you strength upon your broken lands. Gain all to give all, for the Lord God declares the time is now, and the horn of the wicked shall be broken off in all the lands. Let the truth shine as a beacon into the night. For the world shall not pass away until the appointed hour. These are My words, and they shall come to pass. Let your pride go, and follow Me, for these things shall be and are now as we speak."**

As the clouds grow in strength and influence, I know catastrophe awaits within. A peril and panic on Earth from a storm never before known to man—so relentless and terrifying the sun will become darkened. No longer will light give meaning to the coming days, but in our hearts peace and harmony will dwell, manifesting righteousness, and our days will come from the light within us, for the sun shall be darkened and the moon rent in two.

The world will know the time of the Lord is soon at hand, and the glory of the Lord shall be revealed. Before there is thunder, one sees the lightning across the sky. So shall you be in that day when the world is preparing for the sins of the fallen to be forgiven by the Son of God. There shall be every knee and every tongue at the mercy of the Lord, and every heart will descend upon the land into repentance and supplication of good things the Lord shall do for them.

Glorified by all, He will then descend upon the clouds of the sky and deliver His children from this rising storm so vile and dangerous that man will curse the name of God and turn their backs on Him. But our ever merciful God will have patience and call their names one by one. Tearfully but boldly, He will descend upon the Earth the promised judgments, and the storm will pinnacle around Him. He will bring forth a terror in the land and deliver into each day new meaning for newfound believers in Christ. These new soldiers of God shall die by their faith and great honor shall be bestowed in Heaven. Behold! A special place shall be reserved in Heaven for those who die at the will of God and in the name of our Lord Jesus Christ!

They shall praise His name and reach for His hand to ascend into His domain. He will forever dwell with them in the House of the Father. They will walk the land hand in hand with Him, and they will praise His holy name. He shall be glorified by all, and the days will be forevermore.

But only His children will find comfort and protection from the coming storm.

He will avenge those who persecute against Him. He will destroy those who curse His name. He will bestow upon the wicked, so malicious and malignant, a place of torment where no comfort can dwell, and the very air in their lungs will cry out for God's mercy. They will cry to God Almighty to bring comfort and water to cool their scorching tongues. Unable to do anything but be tormented day and night, all those who sailed the wrong way will pay the ultimate price of being caught in the storm. They will not be pardoned in that time, because it will be too late. They will be tortured until the end of the earth and then until the end of time and after. They will grow weary and distressed, never finding comfort nor strength. They will eternally mourn and cry for help, but none will be found. Only in this time will everyone know who the great Almighty God really is.

    He will bind their sins and bring judgment upon the nations. Those who died in His name and by His name will receive heavenly harkening and receive crowns of life and incorruptibility. They shall further feed on the bread of life, and their days will be provided by the light of God Almighty. They shall not grow tired nor weary, because Jesus will bring them comfort and dwell among them. They shall be cooled of all their thirsts and desires, and they shall not be anxious nor worry, because the Spirit of God will let them drink from His living waters, and they shall be satisfied in abundance and forevermore. They will not grow sad nor depressed as Christ will wipe away all their tears. The righteous and believing souls will be commended for their service to the Lord God Almighty and never once will they long for the days to end. They will rejoice in the name of the Lamb, their God, and forever reign with Him in the House of the Father.

But as I sail, I know in my heart the storm is perilous and few will catch it in time. Many will be lost and few will survive. I plead to you for salvation in the Lord so this catastrophe might be averted. We should find strength in Him and each other to live righteous and holy in the eyes of the Lord for His mercy and goodness shall endure. Repentance shall not be freely given for all time, but the time is now. He shall offer, and you shall receive.

"But these things are not freely given," says God, **"for there shall be much work and few will survive."** Let these things be heard, for the voice of God is on the wind, and the times are now. No longer should we let a day pass without seeing the responsibilities of your future as a child of God. There are many who are lost, and the call is now. Do not delay and do not tarry, for these things shall come to pass.

Exalt God and release your pride. One cannot live for God and for man, **"but by every word that comes from the mouth of God"** (Matthew 4:4). My God is a just God and certainly no person living in the passions of this life can be of God and enter His kingdom. In their rebellion they shall be judged and cast into outer darkness where there will be weeping and gnashing of teeth. Judgment will come. I beg you to remain alert and ready for the sleepy souls of the earth shall perish in the storm. Listen and obey—even at the peak of darkness—for we know not what tomorrow brings.

Are you ready for the storm? All you need is faith in God. Believe in your heart and proclaim His glory. Live by His teachings and forever serve the Son of Man. I sail on in my voyage with endurance through the peace of God, and in my heart He dwells day and night. All my faith I put in Him. Gladness fills my soul, and I rejoice in tribulation. The ever so slow drift through time continues, and yet my duties remain unfulfilled.

Star Light

Coasting over open water, the waves caress the bow of my holy vessel. Yearning for the comfort the ocean carries and with its voyage the truth and promise of our coming Lord and Savior Jesus Christ, I search the moonlit sky of a bright and starry night. Light shining from an object of true brilliance and of such great capacity glows of an illumination of life and peace from within.

Wondrous spectacles dance across the sky, shining in the beckoning night, and I long for the presence of my Holy Father. I sit in awe of what miraculous wonders were created by the sea and the promises of His love amidst my soul. These things were shone from a light of such true clarity of nature, given through the hand of God, and His light remains our direction in these perilous times. We were made to show love for others so His love could be sent from Heaven with wondrous grace and great mercy.

In this star-lit shining night of stars so bright, I await the message God has sent me in this time of holy giving and thanks. I praise His holy name and seek wisdom and truth. I long to be more and more like my Almighty God, and I see in Him virtues of which I long to acquire in great and heavy abundance.

I sail on in my voyage not knowing where it takes me but relinquishing all fear and following the wake of heavenly glory. I have raised my flag and declared Jesus as my savior. I sit in the path of an awesome adventure. Knowing only where I am headed, I am not quite sure how someone like me of such utter earthly worthlessness can acquire such beauty and heavenly wonders. By faith I walk in the path of righteousness while gleaming of God's holiness filled throughout my soul. I live for a worthy cause knowing the night will show the way to others in need of their salvation.

I stare at the North Star and its bearing across the great expanse of the sea, and I grasp the complexities of its nature as if it was put there for direction in a time of uncertainty. Its structure formed from three stars and sitting in great majesty across the universe, I sit in awe of this magnificent wonder and everything else seems to fade. Staring at this star, it seems as if God put it there for the purpose of following Him. I know wherever I go and whatever I do, that star remains in its place guiding me. I realize God is the same way. No matter what I do in life, God always remains right there with me. He never moves. Only when I turn my vessel around and sail the wrong way do I lose ground between us, but if I turn around and seek Him in all of His wonder and glory, He'll be right there in front of me—due north.

There is no east and west with God Almighty, only north and south. Either we pick up our cross and follow Him and all of His spiritual blessings are poured out to equip us for the coming times or we sail into the oblivion of utter destruction to be fully encompassed by the storm in our life of evil and deceit. Like the North Star and its light, God's power never fades or fails. He is ever merciful and no matter where you are in your life, He is right there waiting for you to return to Him.

Man was put on earth to serve God, not to enjoy earthly pleasures. To serve God in all His wonder and power is pleasure beyond comprehension or comparison of anything on earth. That's because God is not of this earth, but the earth was made for us to serve Him and praise His holy name. Only when we turn to Him in confession of our sins and begin to follow His commands and plans for our lives do we thereby find entry into the Kingdom of God. **"Every tree that does not bear good fruit is cut down and thrown into the fire. Thus you will recognize them by their fruits"** (Matthew 7:19-20).

Surely no man with evil, deceit, corruption, and hate will be allowed to inherit the heavenly domain God has in store for His children. Only when we ask God to open our spiritual eyes and follow Jesus through the ocean and its rising waves will our holy voyage with God find its course. We must look to God beyond all things. Put Him first in everything you do, and He will bless you all of your days.

The stars are dimming with the dullness of an ever corrupting earth. The days of my voyage are rising in number, but those left ahead are shrinking with each passing hour. Only when we search the sky shall we find that God's love never fails. The star never moves from its position in the darkening night and our holy Jesus Christ never moves one inch from that spot in our hearts once we open it up and let Him into our lives. Filled with amazement and just small tastes of God's holy power, I sail on in this voyage of newfound discovery with purpose and direction and with Jesus as my bright morning star.

As the Clouds Pass By

Emblazoned clouds following a straight and narrow path march through a beautiful sky, and I think of all of the wonderful things my God has done. Though crucified and persecuted, Jesus willingly died on the cross for every sin in each person's life. He arose on the third day and proclaimed victory. Amen!

The Son of God, our Redeemer, gave us His life so we might be saved and dwell with Him in the house of God, and as the sky shows me in this long and amazing voyage, my life on this earth is with purpose and His Spirit has been given to guide, direct, and empower me in these times. When I put myself last, forsook the world, declared Him Lord, and turned my life over to Him, I received the promise of eternal life. Then He bestowed in me purpose and a calling to perform a mighty feat. However it wasn't until I placed my life upon the altar and submitted to His perfect plan did He equip me with the gifts and spiritual empowerment to perform the mission.

Deep inside, everyone on Earth has a gift from God. Only when we receive salvation and put Him first in our life will we truly know what great work God has in store for us. He wants to be glorified through our actions and approach to life—through our interactions with others—and only when we come to terms with His plan for us and His specific expectations will we be truly blessed.

Everyone has a great work to do for the Lord. If we will embrace this truth and ask God to show meaning in our lives, we can then truly understand the voyage we must embark on. We are now living in the very last of days. Everyone must realize that significance, but what most do not seem to acknowledge are the incredible opportunities God has afforded us by being an integral piece of the most pivotal time in history! We are in the climax of God's story for humankind, and we have an obligation to ensure the souls of the greatest spiritual harvest the earth has ever experienced occurs just as God foreknew before the very creation of the world! When we truly embrace that urging we each feel—the call of a lifetime, because we know we were born different and for a special purpose—then we have a chance to survive the devastation ahead.

Only the Father knows when that day will come when He directs Jesus to call together all believers to meet in the clouds, but before that day arrives we will be faced with evil the world has never seen. The times approach when black skies shall be all that is left, but His light shall shine from within and no worries will life cause, because the Lord shall comfort us in the cloud of His protection.

As the storm clouds pass us by and the days wear on, our fellow neighbors of this world will turn their backs on the One they need most. It is our duty as children of God to do all we can through the power given by His Spirit to help guide unbelievers toward Jesus and help them find salvation. The time has come for Christians to set an example for the people of this world and be Christ-like in every word and deed. We must embrace the full Word of God and pray without ceasing. We must throw out all evil with the dogs.

Set your eyes upon Christ and live by His teachings and commands. Humble yourselves as servants of the Most High God and shine the light of Christ by walking in humility and love. Look to the Lord and make every day your mission to emulate His ways by being empty and allowing the Spirit of God to live through you. Our burdens shall be lifted by His mercy and grace, and He will pour out His spiritual blessings in abundance to ready you for the trials ahead.

Our mission on earth does not include anything of earthly pleasure. Our sole purpose is to glorify God by serving Him and to spread the gospel of Jesus Christ to the very ends of the earth. Until the Church unites as one and puts aside each insignificant difference of belief, the Spirit of God is not going to manifest Himself. Forgive one another and seek forgiveness from God with humility and a deep desire for God's perfect plan for your life. God will provide anyone who seeks His Spirit to taste from

His living waters. Our edification comes from the Holy Spirit, and our body should be as a vessel unto God to be poured into at His discretion. Once filled with the Spirit, He can work through us to accomplish the very purposes for which we were created. Allowing Him to work through us will strengthen our faith and resolve, and we will be able to glorify Him in every word and deed. Our actions will be in line with the leading of the Spirit of God and we can truly walk in faith and obedience as we respond to His call.

God's most important lesson for His children is that obedience is crucial—pivotal. The prophet Samuel reflected the attitude of God when speaking to Saul saying, **"Has the Lord as much delight in burnt offerings and sacrifices as in obeying the voice of the Lord? Behold, to obey is better than sacrifice, and to heed than the fat of rams"** (1 Samuel 15:22 NASB).

If God gives direction or purpose with an intent for us to perform and do, release your pride and do what is necessary. If God calls a pastor on a mission to another country, that pastor should not delay the will of God but should perform His plan and purpose to full completion and fruition.

This holy voyage with God on earth will one day end, but our eternal lives with Christ Jesus shall commence and be forevermore. We will rejoice in His name and exalt Him as Lord, singing of His praise and power. Focus on these promises as you suffer for Jesus and the kingdom of God just as those who came before you have suffered. Suffer with joy and sound purpose in your hearts and minds.

As Christians and believers in Jesus, we *must* walk away from the desires and passions for the world. The flesh thrives when the spirit falters. Turn away from sin and turn toward God. Nothing of this world in theory or substance is worth missing the eternal salvation of your soul. Everything we live for should be delegated under the supreme authority of God and with His plan and purpose in mind. Wake up and see the voyage God has for you and your family! Pray to the Almighty God for deliverance and healing today! Repentance and a turning away from the sins of the world are key first steps.

My earthly voyage in pursuit of Him will one day fade away, but the promises of God will never fade away. One day this body will die, and my burdens will be lifted from my heart and soul, but until that time I press on with full intent on overcoming the rough and treacherous seas ahead through the strength in me given by an Almighty God. Then and only then will I accomplish all that I seek.

Are you tired of trying to please the world? God longs for your surrender and submission to His will for your life. All you have to do is realize the world is full of temporary pleasure and short-term fixes. Do you believe Jesus Christ died on the cross for your sins, arose on the third day, and is even now at the right hand of God? Do you confess with your mouth Jesus Christ is Lord and believe in your heart God raised Him from the dead (Romans 10:9)? Do you understand you are a sinner and want to surrender your heart to Jesus Christ as your Savior? Are you willing to do everything in your power to empty yourself so

Christ can live through you? If you are sincere and tired of walking through this world alone and without purpose, fall on the altar and ask Jesus to take control of your life. He will guide you and strengthen you the rest of the way, giving you a peace which surpasses all understanding to guard your hearts and minds in Christ Jesus (Philippians 4:7).

Please pray this simple prayer:

"Jesus, I confess each sin to You today. I know You died for my sins and arose on the third day, thereby through grace and the blood of Your sacrifice my sins will be atoned for and I might be saved. I know You expect a lot from me. Lord, I love You and give you my WHOLE heart, and I lay every ounce of me on the altar to give to You and receive Your purpose for my life. I know I can't take Your love for granted and on this very day, with everything in me, I will begin to live by Your teachings and commandments. I know You are gracious and holy, and I thank You for sparing me from the coming judgment. I love You and thank You for all of Your many blessings. In Your holy, wondrous name I pray, amen."

The time has come to take the call of God seriously. Step forward, and receive your orders and mission from the Almighty, and vow on this very day to not let one moment pass as you press on in fulfillment of His plan. If we don't take our salvation, God's Word, prayer, fellowship, and our entire relationship with Him personally we will never make it to see the wonder and glory He has prepared for us. Believe in the Son of God and surrender fully to Him today. Decide right now to follow Him no matter where His path takes you and be faithful to the call He has placed upon your life.

I love you all, but most importantly, Jesus loves you. Make sure you don't miss out on something worth more than your life in this world. Make it your mission to be one with Christ. Devote your *whole* life to Him and Him alone. Don't just give a part of yourself to Him but all of your being. God doesn't want what you can offer in your spare time or when you need help. God wants you every minute of every day for the rest of your entire life and no less. Embrace His love and come to terms with what He has planned for your life.

In this holy voyage, I embrace the future and all it brings. I long for the everlasting life to come. I watch the clouds in anticipation of the coming glories. My mission and purpose on this earth is at hand, and I accept that sacrifices must be made. Together we will lead as many lost and lonely souls as we can to redeeming salvation. I drift along in this rolling sea of truth and see a multitude of wonders in the distance. My entire being belongs to God, and my purpose shall be fulfilled. As for today, I sail on. This voyage of truth and satisfaction in the Lord continues, and my duties remain unfulfilled.

Deep Inside

Across this sea of everlasting discovery and excitement, I see glimpses of what the next era will bring. Along boundaries of the sky and sea my limits ride on the crests of the bright blue waves, and I breathe a fresh taste of life and salvation. Longing to grow stronger in Him, I believe in my heart that I was put on this earth for the sole purpose of bringing the lost sheep home to their Shepherd. I search my inner-self wondering and praying for God to show me the most effective and quickest way, but I am assured there is enough time. God promises that all of His human creation will have a chance to taste His power and wonder. His Spirit will manifest in ways the world has never seen.

My eyes scan the surrounding sea, and I know my job is to fish for the Lord and reel in as many souls as possible. He assures me and gives me confidence that although some fish live in the deeper waters and are harder to reach and bring in, He will make my line longer, stronger, and appealing to fish all kinds. Below the waves of bitter deceit, fish hide from the predators of the deep longing for the food of life. Searching desperately for the one truth that can fill the gap or missing piece in their heart, they need only the Word of God and His promises. Then they too shall be sent out to fish for the souls of man and fight for the glory of God through prayer and supplication as members of His mighty army.

As I sail onward in this journey of knowledge and truth, I am assured of the full power of God's endless mercy and love. Race and upbringing do not matter. Income and what side of town you are from do not matter. Background and past forgiven sins do not matter. We have all failed and fallen short of the glory of God (Romans 3:23), but those who are His have been lifted up and renewed (Psalms 51:10; Romans 12:2; 2 Corinthians 4:16; Ephesians 4:23)—strengthened with true purpose by the Holy Spirit of the Almighty God on High. Step forward and accept His truths for you today. Fall on your knees, exalt the God of all creation, and obey His every word upon your heart. Then His Spirit shall heal your wounds and strengthen your hearts for tomorrow.

Even after man curses His name and spits on His work, God still provides endless mercy, and His undying love and devotion never fails. Repentance is all that is necessary to begin the process of having that hole in your heart completely filled. Not only will He heal your shattered heart and sanctify you inside and out, He will allow you to drink from living waters and be satisfied in abundance. Only after these things have been accomplished in your life can you fully grasp the power of God.

His full power is incomprehensible. He is mighty and wondrous and loves all of His children. His love is as deep and as wide as the ocean. I look down over the edge of my holy vessel, and I gaze out through the holy waters of God. I stand in awe and amazement at how something put on Earth can serve so many purposes. God created His children in the same way. He wants each and every one of His believers and followers to serve Him and praise His mighty name, but He also has a plan beyond your calling. Part of the calling of every child of God is to raise up other spiritual warriors and disciples of God, strengthen them through unity in the Spirit, and send them out to be a force multiplier.

God requires unity in the body of Christ during the coming times for His Spirit to move as He intends. Gather together in truth and purpose to work together in leading unbelievers back to Him in the manner of which they are called. God makes it known through His Word that we are to be fishers of men, and He is waiting for all His people to gather together before He sends His Son in glorious power and wonder. God is holding back because of His endless mercy. He knows there are many fish searching desperately for the food of life, and He wants us as His fishermen to drop the nets and bring in full loads. Put another way, as His servants we are to ready His crop. The harvest cannot wait. The season draws near!

Even during the storm we should never quit fishing, but we are to bring truth, hope, and understanding in a time of darkness and deception. We should cast out the nets and bring in as many as time will allow. Then, *and only then*, we can know in our hearts that God will honor us for our efforts. We should send out boatloads of fishermen and cast out the biggest nets our holy vessels are able to carry. But while fishing, God will turn our boats into mighty ships, extend our lakes to rivers, and our rivers to oceans. He will bless immeasurably in each effort.

We must work through the weather even though the storm will become strong and dangerous. We will find strength and peace from the storm in our Lord and Savior, Jesus Christ. He will bind together His people, and the storm won't penetrate but will cease in power and retreat to strengthen where evil dwells. It will be like a hurricane moving over land. The unbelieving will flee from its confusion and deceit only to be caught in the storm and perish in its void of total darkness. But the pure and holy believers of God will take refuge in the Lord Jesus Christ, and the storm will pass them by, not penetrating the strongest and most righteous at heart. But they will live to see God's holy power and divine tranquility. They will grow in faith by praise and worship, and their lives will be blessed by putting them in the hands of the Lord.

His endless love never fails, but He can only reach out and knock on the door. You must then be willing to open the door and invite Him in. His undying devotion renders something the pleasures of this earth can never offer. He offers refuge from the storm. Will you accept His invitation? You must relinquish your pride of this world and seek Him.

I drift along in a peace that will see me through the storm, but I know there will be more fishing up ahead. I gather my nets for the Lord God is my master and friend. I long for His comfort and blessings, but work is at hand. He expects undying devotion and a full boatload.

I praise His mighty name and thank Him for His wonderful and undying love and devotion in my life. Without Him I am nothing, but with Him I am everything, because He is everything. My faith I put in the Lord Jesus Christ. He is my navigator and my captain. He leads me on the straight and narrow path of righteousness for His name's sake. I exalt Him on high and thank Him for the call upon my life and blessings within my soul. I continue on in this voyage knowing it won't always be smooth, calm waters. I raise my sail and look to Him for strength and power in getting through the storm with more work accomplished and more sinners washed clean of their transgressions. The aspects of my life are understood, and yet my duties remain unfulfilled.

Strength from the Sun

As I sail on in this everlasting journey with my Almighty Gracious Father, I know in my heart we are going to one day be together in His home of heavenly dwelling and wondrous power. But as this world ventures on in the current pace of growing corruption and evil, I fall to my knees in prayer. In a world long forgotten, He created the souls of man, and they created the way to destruction in their wake. Now those who have not been born again live in bondage to the sinful flesh, the flesh weak and the spirit heavy without the uplifting power of God to breathe new life.

Here and now, the sins of the sons of man have ravaged all of humankind, and their treachery has extended to the outermost corners of the earth. God, in His wisdom, created man, and through His mercy gave His Son to die for man so that lost and uncaring souls could find redemption and salvation despite their sinful natures.

Boldly before the throne of grace, I pray for great mercy for these lost and damaged souls and for salvation to be poured upon the ungodly. I long for the grace of God to comfort the weary and to provide strength to the hearts of the broken and beaten. Knowing I will one day come face to face with my God and answer for my life's work, I seek to serve Him and complete His plan for my life.

The call goes forth for God's children to find their purpose and work out their **"own salvation in fear and trembling"** (Philippians 2:12 KJV), **"holding forth the word of life; that [they] have not run in vain, neither labored in vain"** (Philippians 2:16 KJV). **"Do all things without murmurings or disputing, that ye may be blameless and harmless, the sons of God, without rebuke, in the midst of a crooked and perverse nation, among whom ye shine as lights in the world."** (Philippians 2: 14-15 KJV).

Longing to see Him in all His glory, I am compelled to leave this world and rejoice in His heavenly domain. My journey is just beginning, but I need strength to carry on in this hate-filled and corrupted world. I search the sky and am blinded by the sun's searing light and ever-growing heat. I search my heart for answers and realize in my searching that God is akin to all of His creations. He is one with the universe. He lives among us and fills every moment of every day with His love and divine power. I long for His empowerment so that I might do His work. I know that without His help and strength I won't be able to make it through these terrible times. I would falter and fail in my duties. I struggle for understanding, but soon I know the sun is the key to my lesson on strength in Him.

As I gaze blindly into the sun, I know God is like the sun in that He shines His power and light upon the world each and every day, but in some places darkness lingers where the presence and power of God is not found. Even in the dark of night, the sun is trying to work its way back to those regions, but the sleepy souls of man rest quietly in their passions for the world. There is no desire for the morning, and they linger in the shadows of destruction. **"So shall it be in the end,"** says the Lord.

Every moment, God's Spirit reaches out to forgive, but the souls of man must repent and ask for the redemption they don't deserve but freely receive. Not one second does He quit but is eternally reaching out, working in people's lives, and touching the unsaved. He offers His power and strength to those desperate to glorify Him. He abundantly pours out His Spirit to those who yearn for the quiet touch of God. Although we don't always render our hearts faithfully to Him, He always accepts everything we have to offer. He perpetually gives us His blessings, everlasting and filling, but He wants our whole hearts.

Only when the children of God turn from His ways and live for the world and those that rule the world does the fire of God's wrath burn bright. The sun swells and blazes onto the deck of my vessel showing that He is the Almighty God, and that He will not be overcome by anyone or anything. His wrath will be poured out in due time, and the world will be in awe of His power and long for just a breath of chance to be spared, but they in that time shall be quenched out by the hand of God's fury upon the world. His wrath shall be poured out from the hands of His angels, and the fury of God shall spare none. The time for chances and opportunity will have passed and the price for the sins and corruption of the wicked shall be paid out through death and burning annihilation. The fire burns bright and nothing but judgment shall prevail in that time.

The Almighty God shall not be toyed with, for He will bring vengeance on all people who have defiled themselves in the lusts of the world. The world will not last, but the Kingdom of God shall be eternal. He will pour strength upon His people, and He will lessen their loads, because they exalt His name and carry out His will. They walk toward the plans of God and forsake all they know so that they might know someone far greater. They have relinquished their pride of the world and uplift Jesus Christ. They carry their crosses with humility in their hearts and joy on their faces. They are different, and they know it. Called to special purpose, they are the generation of warriors of which God foreknew and the prophets foretold, and they shall usher in the reign of the King.

Step forward and believe in your purpose during this time. Hear the call of God's voice on the wind and feel the heat from inside your soul and *know with every single ounce inside of you that you were created for* **this very moment.**

The children of God shall be persecuted and die for the glory of God. Such is the reality of the call. War brings forth death and destruction, but you shall rise up and live in eternity! What purpose could be more significant—more permanent and lasting? The power of God burns bright within you. What darkness can stop the glory of God from flowing through His willing vessels? **"He will guard the feet of his faithful ones, but the wicked shall be cut off in darkness, for not by might shall a man prevail"** (1 Samuel 2:9).

He will raise us up, and the feet of His warriors will walk steady and true, never stumbling or faltering from the path set before us, and the words and wisdom of God shall prevail in the darkness. His voice will call to us, and He will guide us through the night. The winds shall howl and the world will burn with fire and pillars of smoke, but the darkness will fall before us leading us into the new wonders of God. The souls of many shall be won from the darkness, and the voice of God shall thrust us into the manifest glory of His power and greatness.

He only wants us to love Him the way He loves us and for us to follow Him wherever He goes. His will is the only way, and only His obedient children see the light at the precipice of the darkness. For each one walks in rank and file, one by one and two by two, and each carry no burdens and shoulder no loads, but inside and from within them, the light of God shines forth into the world. Their solemn vows shall give each a new promise for tomorrow, and the souls of the lost and weary shall be renewed into new promise for the days ahead. Each shall follow in purpose and plan, and the glory of God shall be revealed in each. The days ahead are vast but few in number, and the world shall grow in evil and great deceit, but the tireless trek through the unknown continues—the voice of God directing each at every step on every path forward.

His plan is perfect, and His purpose shall be fulfilled. Let your voice be heard as the voice of God speaks through you. Let your words be spoken in wisdom and truth and allow the glory of God to shine as strength from the sun onto a darkened morning. The sun shall rise, and the darkness shall falter, and all shall be revealed that was once in darkness. Let those who have ears hear the good news! The voice of God speaks within each of us and the days ahead are those made for the purpose of God in mind and the plan of the few to fulfill. Set your feet upon the path with purpose and great conviction. Lay your bodies upon the altar of God, for you will suffer in the world, and the world will hate you. You will be persecuted and know pain. But your rewards will be in Heaven, and you will know the honor of God forever.

As I sail on in this voyage with God, I know that the days ahead are the hardest I have ever faced, but I know the glory of God and His strength within my Spirit. He knows me, and He knows what I can handle. His purpose for my life is perfect, and I shall walk forward with this purpose of fulfillment and obedience to the call. My life I have put into the hands of the Lord, and I will not lower my gaze nor falter in the faith.

My God keeps me in all things, and His words are ever faithful. He is my teacher and my inspiration. None other is greater than He, and His strength lives in me and fuels the fire within my heart, so that others may see the lamp which burns onto my path. The darkness shall not touch me, but He shines brightly through me so others might escape from bondage.

I seek the day of Your coming, oh Lord, but I remember Your teachings and live by Your Word. I hope that others will follow my example as I follow Yours set forth through Your Word and that my actions will not bring shame to Your holy name. I pray these words will exalt Your wondrous presence in a world of bitter deceit and hate. I love You Lord, and Your work in my life amazes me each and every day. Though I am unworthy, You have given me so much promise. I praise you, oh God. You are my Savior and my strength. My voyage continues forward toward the task at hand. The aspects of my life are understood, and yet there are duties to be fulfilled.

A Breath of Life

Though the days are numbered, the breath of God breathes new life into my tomorrow and beyond. These words are the few with which I am guided and are my commands toward the coming battles. The voice of God gives His strict instruction, and I shall not be moved.

The times are coming when we shall gather together with one voice. The Spirit of God will descend upon all the earth and the few will stand ready to gather the ones who have been chosen for the task. These are the elect, and they shall set their feet upon the proper course. Take heed to the days for the night swiftly approaches. Follow the words of the Lord, and He shall maneuver you through all situations.

The night approaches, but you shall be ready as lights and beacons in the darkness. The fire will fall and the manna of

Heaven will be given to God's obedient. Listen and obey, and His voice will ring true in your spirits. Let your hearts be at peace, for the God of your salvation shall take you up and prevent you from the coming disaster, but there must be a quickening first. The Spirit of God will blow in like an east wind, and the fire of Heaven will consume the enemy. The children of God shall rejoice, and many shall be saved. But many shall also fall away, and these shall persecute and kill you. Take heed for the coming of the age is upon us. There will be terror and stricken hearts upon the landscape, but the pure in heart shall prevail in all things, for they have kept themselves true to the will of God, and He has cast his seal upon their foreheads.

The Word of God is your weapon. Wield it in times when the enemy shall approach you in the form of light. For light shall only stand in light, and the darkness cowers in the presence of the Lord. The Word of God discerns and determines all things, and the spirits of darkness shall have no power over you. Let your voice be heard. Cast them out, and proclaim the power of Jesus over them. Let your voice be heard, and the darkness shall flee from you.

I awaken to a new day provided by God for all of humankind to receive their instruction. The moving of the waves motion the time is at hand, and the nets must be cast into the water. I study the surrounding ocean and the waves which carry it and know there exists a meaning under the surface not yet gathered. I breathe in the fresh morning breeze, and the power of my God overwhelms me. He breathes life into His creations, and

His Spirit guides the steps of the broken. A lowly sort, God's warriors step forward into the darkness with the light of God before them. Demons scurry, and the darkness flees, but the storm rages forth anew.

Breathe in the Spirit of the Lord, and know you are of great importance to Him. Receive the Holy Spirit. Seek strength in Him. Long for the River of Life so you may be filled in abundance. Fast and pray, being obedient to God, and gain His favor. Live day by day in sight of what is to come. Obedience is greater than sacrifice. King David earned favor through obedience to the will of God by being faithful to His commands.

The surrounding earth hums a tune of God's holy power, and I long to be filled with His virtues and glory. I find strength in You, oh Lord. You are my Rock and my Fortress. I stand in Your name, and I love You with my whole heart. Gracious and mighty are Your blessings upon me and my family. I long to be home in Your holy presence, but my understanding has begun to bloom like flowers in the spring. No longer shall the world have an effect on my life, but I will do everything to glorify Your holy, precious name. You are wondrous and mighty, oh Jesus. I bow in awe and humbleness, because You are the Light of my Life. You lead my paths straight and bright.

I continue forward with the battle plans for the coming days, and God shows me the face of the earth. I know the mission is perilous, and there is much work ahead. There are few for the task but many shall be reaped in the harvest. Know in your soul that He is at work.

Set aside the things of the world, and **"seek ye first the kingdom of heaven and His righteousness, and all these things shall be added unto you"** (Matthew 6:33 KJV). Long to be close to God. Walk in His power and by His grace He will equip you for the coming time and lead you into the domain of everlasting life. Remain holy and steadfast in the Lord so you may find favor in His eyes. Walk every day of your life in the light of Jesus Christ, thanking Him for the sacrifice He made at the cross. We must increase our knowledge and faith in Him. The days continue to grow in evil and deception, and we can no longer allow ourselves to mesh with the world and compromise God's calling in our lives. Those who have ears let them understand.

Unite! Band together in the name of Jesus. Set aside your differences and beliefs. Place your faith in Jesus Christ and let Him breathe new life and move throughout the world in front of you. Stretch out your hands and believe, and the Spirit of God will move mountains before you. Have faith and trust in Him. Speak, and it shall be done. Receive, and it shall prosper. Live in sight of all He has provided, and know that He is coming soon. Continue in all things with the promise of His return. Pursue the Heavenly things, and this life shall pass before you and birth greater rewards in the resurrection.

This voyage with God is devoted to God's work. I look toward the horizon and see the Strength which holds my heart, and I long to feel His presence. I know in my heart that I must grow closer to the Lord and seek His face. I want to know my Savior, Jesus Christ. He is my Light and my Strength. He is the

Rock on which I stand each and every day. His Spirit resides in me, and I know that He will strengthen in times of distress, aid in times of confusion, bring comfort in times of sadness, and show compassion to those who seek His face.

I worship the Holy name of Jesus and give thanks for His blessings, but I know in my heart that we are on the verge of a holy war. Know your part and accept it. Remember to keep Him and His name holy in all that you do and glorify Him in your words and deeds.

I sail on in this venture to be one with You, Jesus, but I must be steadfast in all I do, remaining holy in Your eyes. I have seen the trail I must take and thank You for Your blessings. My eyes are upon You, and I long to glorify Your name. The aspects of my life are understood, but there is still much work to be done.

Power and Praise

Holy and divine is the Lord. He creates in me a peace from the world and a refuge from my enemies. He glorifies and strengthens in all that He does. I long to be just like Him. I seek to be close to Him and one day witness the treasures stored up for those who are obedient to His will.

Thus far on my voyage with God, I have encountered many teachings. I have embraced His anointing along the way and more fully understand the duties to which I have been called. They are without choice and with great purpose. Lean into His promise, oh people of heavy hearts! Let the joy of God surround your hearts with peace and thanksgiving!

I put my faith in the Lord and draw strength from Him each day. I worship His holy name, and I long for the people of God to open their eyes and passionately seek Him. Put your faith in the Lord so you might receive His eternal blessings and promises. Long for the Bread of Life. Live by faith that He will take care of you, and believe He is watching over you. In whatever happens, the Lord God will protect you from all of the evil the world carries.

Never quit seeking His face, and always put your faith in Him. Chase God, and you will receive from Him blessings even without asking. So first seek the kingdom of Heaven in all that you do, and He will provide all of your necessities. For the Lord, our God, is a merciful God. He is a just God. Dare not question His authority, but live in sight of things to come and accomplish what is expected of you. Then the following days will bring forth prosperous fruit and the unyielding and divine power of God throughout the earth.

It is time we release our opinions and pride of the world and lift our hands to the heavenly domain of Jesus, our Lord and Savior, and cry in His name:

> *"Jesus! Jesus! Bring forth the glory of the Living God. Jesus! I weep in sadness for the sins of this world, but I rejoice in Your promises! Thank You! Pour out Your mighty wonder and glory and cleanse me of all my transgressions. Jesus! Praise be to the Almighty Living God. Just and righteous are Your ways in all that You do.*

I sing throughout the heavens and the earth a new song! You are my safe haven. You are my resting place. My body is a temple unto You, oh Lord. I praise Your mighty name, though I trek through this corrupted land. Bring forth your will, oh Lord! I seek You in all that I do, and for all of the days of my life, I will carry my cross. I follow in Your path of glory and righteousness."

Believe in the power of God to transform this world we live in. The persecution of Christians throughout the world grows and children are dying with the name of Jesus Christ on their lips. Praise God for the blessings and honor they shall receive in Heaven! But stand in the light of knowledge, understanding that we must fight back through much prayer and fasting. Rise up from the dust, spiritual warriors! Fast and seek God! Pray without ceasing, in all things glorifying His name. Rise up in the purposes of God, knowing you are obedient to Him no matter what He commands. Bow in humility and humble yourselves before the Lord.

Speak truth to your transgressors, even in light of growing persecution. Plant the seeds of salvation in the hearts of all, for the Lord desires that all be saved (1 Timothy 2:4), but do not forsake the testimonies of which you have been called. Live your life as one of testimony and servitude to Jesus, performing in obedience to God's commands with a humble heart and contrite spirit (Isaiah 57:15). For the glory of God shall prevail and the words you speak shall go forth and divide the darkness from the light and prosper in its purpose.

God has set aside a different people with a special purpose, and this journey begins with you! He wants His children to believe in Him and have faith instead of listening to their own feelings and opinions. The world births unbelief, but all things are possible through the Spirit of God. Renew your faith, and allow your life to be empowered through dedication to your purpose in this life. Seek Him and all that He offers. Ask, and you shall receive. Seek, and you shall find. Knock, and the door shall be opened unto you (Matthew 7:7; Luke 11:9-10). Appreciate His love and spread the news of His grace and great mercy. Seek to glorify God in all your works while humbling yourselves before the Lord. Remain in humility, and He will raise you up. Whoever desires to be the least of all shall be the one He raises up (Luke 9:48).

How many of you would sacrifice your lives for people who hate you? Would you die for someone who spit in your face? How far would you go for someone else to live? Jesus died so we might live. He shed His own blood for the people of this Earth so that His blood might symbolize His love for all people. He longs for you to go to Him with a desperate heart and a desire to please Him. Every time you do something in His name truly you are blessed, because it is written that blessed are those **"who do not turn away because of me"** (Matthew 11:6 NLT). He will bless you for finding strength in Him. He will speak through you as a vessel of the Lord.

Praise God during the good times and the bad! Praise God in the storm and during the perilous journey through the valleys, for during these times God's presence is most abundant. God loves a desperate heart that remains faithful to Him and praises His name even during times of great testing, persecution, and affliction, for the darkness seeks to steal, kill, and destroy, but we have been set free from the bondages of sin and death and redeemed before an Almighty God who promises to get us through each and every situation (John 10:10; Romans 8:2). Praise God when your spirit abounds and when it mourns. Pray and glorify God in your affliction, for He promises great rewards in Heaven. Seek God in all situations, and then you shall be lifted up and protected from the coming times. Praise God for His promises over your life, for surely the time will come when we shall cast off these mortal bodies and meet our Maker in the heavens above. Pray for that day to come soon.

Blessed be the glory of God. Live for the Lord, and seek to impress Him throughout your daily journey in life. Have faith that you might grow stronger in Him every minute of the day. Long to grasp His heart with spiritual fervor and obedience. But heed my words. Keep the Lord in your sight. Do not look away just because the oceans roar and the waves crash and tumble through the bow of your vessel. God will get your through. Look to Jesus, and He will calm the storm of your heart, even when the world around you has lost all sense of right and wrong. Seek Him in all that you do so that He might make your paths straight. There is no greater love than His, and He gave His life so we might be set free (John 15:13). Praise God!

Jesus, I praise Your name. My soul is filled with the benevolence of a holy and divine embracement of Your love. I long for the day when Heaven will open up and pour out all that is therein. Bring your people back to You, oh Lord. I love You Jesus. I sail on in pursuit of those promises for my life, and I know You will direct my path every step of the way.

His majesty reigns forever and ever. His great love for all people abounds. I continue with strength and fortitude. Harden my will toward the world, but soften my heart in great love and compassion for the lost, Lord Jesus. Give me power to carry on in Your will alone. I submit myself wholeheartedly to You and the mission at hand. I give you all of me for Your glory, oh God.

I glorify the name of Jesus Christ through any and all situations, and I know my God will get me through. See the zeal of God carried through the breeze and know His mercy remains for all to receive and prosper from. His love never fails. I seek to live as an example to all so that you might, "**follow my example as I follow the example of Christ**" (1 Corinthians 11:1). I pray brothers and sisters of God that you don't waver in your voyage, but keep your sails raised, and the wind of the Almighty God will move you into His guiding light. Continue in sight of all that is to come. Glorify His name. The aspects of our lives are understood, and yet our duties remain unfulfilled.

Vivid Scenes

Along the sky's edge, displaying great power and glory, the dawn of day reaches up through the sky and touches down upon all the Earth its radiance and wonder. Elusive and denying are the people who once knew this power but fled from its presence to find comfort in their desires as though they were fleeing into their homes from the heat. Translucent, yet more powerful than the day itself, the works of my Almighty God render a reverent fear in the eyes of His followers and shed respect on the One who created us by His own freewill. As for me in this voyage, I know where I stand with Christ. I know my limits are beyond the stars themselves, and the works we shall have through Christ's name are to be beyond boundaries no man can comprehend.

Most people at some point in their lives seek the Almighty God to feel out what He has to offer. They want the abundant love of God to overwhelm them with radiant wonder. People want His love to bring them to a changing point in their lives where they might get over that biggest hurdle. They want Him to provide the solutions to their life's problems. They pray and seek God, and He hears their cries because He loves all His creation. He may even provide help, but soon the cries fade and many people return to their sinful lives and forget about Him completely until the time is right and the problems have once again grown with the rising seas around them.

Still, some want a real change in their lives and need God's help to get there. They are tired of living in the sin around them. The world has beaten them to a point of submission, and there's only one direction left to look. So they look up and search for God and true meaning in their lives, and then He reaches down with mercy and touches them with peace and a joy beyond measure.

How about you? Do you want God to change your life? Prayer, while important, is only one piece of the puzzle. Beyond the clouds above is more sky and across the sky are yet more clouds. Prayer is like one piece of an extremely large puzzle while God is telling you where the pieces go. But many don't want to listen to His words and convictions. We seek His help, but we don't want to accept what is also expected from us. We want to put the puzzle together, but we want God to do it for us. When He does, we oftentimes aren't satisfied with the results.

God's love is endless, but only when we come to terms with His expectations of us do we see the results in life we long for. I seek to walk with the Lord, but I can't expect Him to carry me at all times. I must search for strength in Him but walk the steps on my own. When my feet falter, He is faithful to catch me and carry me the rest of the way. God won't just pick you up and plop you down atop Mount Everest. You have to climb. Even Jesus had to face the desert, but He was not alone and neither are we.

We are like babies learning to walk. When we first start, we may make it a few feet or across the room, but eventually we fall. In the same way one might catch their child as they fall, the Lord will catch us and put us back on our feet again. But God also expects us to eat and drink and grow. We eventually walk on our strength before finally running! **"Have you not known? Have you not heard? The Lord is the everlasting God, the Creator of the ends of the earth. He does not faint or grow weary; his understanding is unsearchable. He gives power to the faint, and to him who has not might he increases strength. Even youths shall faint and be weary, and young men shall fall exhausted; but they who wait for the Lord shall renew their strength; they shall mount up with wings like eagles; they shall run and not be weary; they shall walk and not faint"** (Isaiah 40:28-31 ESV). Once again, God feeds us, but we must choose to eat and grow stronger so we can one day walk on our own strength.

If I take one extra step before crumbling to my knees then my rewards for that extra step will be reaped in coming times, because my strength will be carried over. I will be able to walk that much further the next time. But I only walk with God through prayer and fasting, faith, and by eating the bread of the Word of God and drinking from His Holy Spirit.

God provides the necessities to each according to their abilities. In each place and time, the bounty of God is given for those who need the answers to their life's question. But those who seek God are given a new thing, one of God and only then shall we know the glory of His promise. These we do not have from the start and must seek through prayer and fasting and through obedience to the will of God. Let those who have ears listen to the wisdom of God!

We only gain wisdom, knowledge, discernment, and understanding through growth in our relationship with the Lord. He provides the needs, but we must have the desire and determination to withstand all temptation through His strength. The help you need shall be there, but you must depend on yourself in addition to God to get through the darkness. Ask Him to equip you with the resilience and strength you need. He is ever faithful, and His promises endure.

Let Him lead you to that place of peace. Follow Him, and don't ask, "Where must I go Father?" Instead say, "Wherever you go Lord, there I will be." He will lead and guide you in your trek through life, and you shall know the promises of God within you. You will be strengthened along the way. He will make your paths straight while your life is crooked, backward, and upside down, and He shall show His glory to each in their own time. He will provide. **But first you must seek Him.** Seek the will of God, and everything else shall be provided (Matthew 6:33).

Depend solely on God, but also depend upon yourself to remain right where God needs you. God doesn't move. He stays in one place. You must depend upon yourself to get closer to Him and become more dependent on your actions to be what God would have them be and not what worldly desires request. For the promises of God are two-fold. One must be obedient to His Word and stand fast in His promise that God will help you endure in any and every situation (Philippians 4:11-13).

When we realize we are one in unity with Christ, we can then come to accept what God expects from us just as we expect from God. Don't ask God to do all of the work for you. Your sacrifice and freewill to do His work will bring spiritual blessings and rewards if you just continue with the covenant you have with Him.

Does anyone know what eternity really means? A hundred years of pleasure on earth is not worth eternity in the lake of fire. But a hundred years of pain and persecution will always be worth the glory and rewards we shall reap from our eternal walk with God. We may not be worthy or glorified through the eyes of man, but God sees and knows our heart. If you seek the Lord with a whole and purified heart and with the desire to find favor in His eyes, your rewards will manifest before God. Man is not worthy of God's endless and abounding love, but by His grace and great mercy we are sanctified and atoned for by the ultimate sacrifice He paid on Calvary. Through the power and glory of the Holy Spirit, God renders His love indescribably to all creatures upon the earth. Reach up and accept all that this promise holds in store for us.

We must begin to realize the extent of God's love for His children. Even though the world curses His name and spits on His image, His endless mercy cries into the night to wait just a little longer! He is still waiting for the desire of one young man or woman to catch His heart through their overwhelming love for Him that they alter His thinking and bring forth the overwhelming power of His manifest glory on something otherwise destined for His wrath.

God holds the entire universe in synchronization to His purpose. When it rains it's from God and is for a purpose. Maybe that one person with a flight delay comes across a minister in the airport and finds salvation through the grace of God and the blood of Jesus Christ. *To God, the storm is always worth the future harvest.* The destruction only finds the unprepared, and **nothing** shall stop the harvest from occurring at the appointed time.

God doesn't want to see any of His creations judged, but by our own freewill do we serve Him. For those willing to serve, do not ask in return. By His love and mercy shall we be spared from the great disaster, that great day of the Lord, but we shall be joined with Jesus and forever reign with Him in unity. Search your heart. Whether it be that you are overwhelmed by the work God is expecting of you or you just do not think you can go on any longer in this world without help, God still loves you, and He wants to help. All things are possible through Christ. No job is too big or too small for Him. My faith in Him swells like the wind in an ever-growing storm. I only need to orient myself in the direction that I am to go, and I will see the sails move and the clouds float by at my back.

The luscious flowers of the spring bring forth prosperity and the beauty of future rewards we shall reap in our efforts to please Him. My eyes are fixed on Him so that I might see those future spring flowers. But yet ahead comes forth the harshest storm ever known to man. If we can make it through the weather, we will see the harvest on the other side. I sail on in this voyage of discovery and exhilaration. Not only do the winds show favor to my sails but aid in my travels and strengthen my vessel.

I give thanks to the One who created it all for the sole purpose of glorifying His precious name. Set your sails, and follow the clouds of our Almighty Savior who loves you dearly. Your name rings in His ear waiting for the chance to shout it out to the angels. Let the shout be heard. Rejoice in the Lord for He has made you whole.

PART TWO
PREPARING GOD'S ARMY

Holy Divine

Powerful as the skies above, the inerrant words of God run through this holy temple built from the inside out to glorify His name and bring His followers to that appointed place of gathering and preparation. Though my voyage has continued with the almighty teachings of Jesus, our Lord and Savior, I still heed the call He gave when I first began. To carry on in His work I must first be willing to listen to all that I have received through God's Word and keep myself from **not one word** of His teachings.

The key to understanding is listening to the voice of God when it spouts within your soul. Listen to the power of the Holy Spirit moving in your spirit, and let His convictions carry you where you need to be. Receive all that He has given and accept His words as infallible truth to be obeyed no matter the cost. Do not worry about the condemnation given through the mouths of the confused and wayward children, but instead **stand up** for what the Lord has shown, and follow His direction given. Do not let man nor Satan discourage you but remain steadfast in the Lord and keep your eyes upon Him at all times.

Above the sky and far beyond there lies a place where everyone seems to want to go, but most do not want to do what it takes to get to there—that wonderful place beyond the clouds. I urge you, fellow Christians, to remain steadfast on the path of righteousness. Do not veer to the right or to the left, but remain upon God's path for your life. Follow Him, and let Him lead you to where you need to be. Do not ever put a limit on following God, but keep the goal in your heart to become closer with Him with every passing hour of the day. Let the power of His holy wonders astound and amaze all that come near.

Remain a willing vessel for the Lord, for He will reward you for your sacrifices. Don't let the unbelieving and evildoers lead you astray, but keep your eyes upon Jesus and seek first the kingdom of God. Remain faithful. Stay in His plans, and let Him fill you with the power of His Holy Spirit. Render your heart to Jesus. Let the voice of God ring true to the depths of your spirit at every minute of the passing day and seek His face in all that you do. Stand up for what you believe in and continue in His work with humility in your heart and joy on your face, because in all that you do, you know that one day you will be rewarded for your efforts as a humble follower and minister of Jesus Christ.

Along the shore's edge there remains predators waiting to devour anyone weary and weak from the voyage. Seek strength from the Son of God. Let Him be your light, and follow Him all of the days of your physical life, because you rejoice and know in your heart that you will reign with Him in Heaven forever and ever.

Beyond the waves of the sea I see yet more waves, and I feel the glory of God flowing through the ocean's air. I stand in awe and wonder how a God so glorious and powerful could love someone as worthless and broken as me.

I search the sky for answers, and yet there seems to be only one explanation for the wonderful and gracious love of God. Though Jesus was born as man and saw and faced the hardships of the world, He remained perfect in the eyes of God. A sinless person on earth and holy and divine in Heaven, He gave the perfect example for all Christ-followers to pursue by way of brokenness and humility before men. But though He walked the earth as man, in His heart He knew what the Father expected from Him and what many throughout the years would take for granted.

Jesus Christ was persecuted, rejected and beaten, spit on, lashed, cursed, laughed at, mocked, and worst of all, hung on a cross with a thorn bush for a crown. Why? Because He loved us unconditionally. The words to describe God's love are impossible to fully capture and wholly articulate. Thousands have followed with beautifully written prose to explain His depth of love for humans, but the true essence cannot be thoroughly captured. He loves us more than anything else He ever created. The earth will die along with the animals and the trees, the ocean and the grass, but our souls have been washed and cleansed by the blood of Jesus and saved through the grace of our God, and His power and conviction through the Holy Spirit gifts us eternal life.

He shows us the deep and powerful levels of love that flow through His veins. His whole being is filled with it. Eternal and wonderful is the great love of God, and all we must do is pick up our cross and follow the One who created us from the dust of the field. Gracious and heavenly is the holy and divine power of the Almighty. He perpetually provides us edification and strength through His Holy Spirit. He works in us and leads us closer to Him if we allow Him the full control to move. If you are willing to give up all you have, give your life to Him, and put yourself in

His hands, He will take care of the rest. You need not worry. Put your faith in Him, and He will lead you the rest of the way.

The grapes of the Holy Spirit's vines are lush and ready to be plucked. Pluck them from the vine, and use them as He instructs. The will of God shall be as He intends. The gifts of God are stored in Heaven above for those who are willing and able to begin their journey and complete the calling He has appointed. I long to be in His holy presence for all eternity, but to see the converted given over to His abundant love makes me want to wait just a little while longer so that I might have more fellow brothers and sisters in Christ joined through His wonderful love. I rejoice in His holy name and seek guidance from Him. I long to be in His perfect will and to be rewarded handsomely and proudly by my Father. He longs to give, but we must be willing to receive. We must be willing to not abuse our gifts but to use them as the Almighty God determines according to His purpose.

We must follow Him no matter the cost so we are not caught in the whirlwind of Satan's deception, evil, and earthly corruption. He longs to twist our minds and possess us with his evildoings. But I long to dwell in the house of the Lord forever and see Satan burn in the eternal lake of burning fire and sulfur. Only then will he know that his work was in vain. He knows he is defeated yet his foolish stupidity leaves him desperately trying to win the war. Please don't let him carry you there with him.

Stand for what you believe in and listen to the conviction of the Holy Spirit. Remain strong and true. As it says in Psalms 26, we are to allow the Lord to examine us and prove us. Let Him test us so we may know that we have been tried and proven. Allow Him to speak through you. Remain in His sight, and great things will come. Look to the sky, and you shall see the awesome power of God. He will guide you in all situations, but first you must walk in His presence with humbleness and humility. Listen to the voice of the Almighty God. Speak His name to unbelievers in a loud voice and show your thanks for what He has given you.

Our Lord and Savior Jesus Christ died for us, and we should always remain faithful and open to the words of His convicting Spirit. The coming times will be hard and devastating. Take refuge from the storm, and let Him take care of you. Let your faith in Him grow with the passing hours. Though once weakened and broken, the Lord strengthens our vessel. He keeps us strong and true—always pressing forward—so opposing winds cannot affect the workings of our Almighty God. Our voyage grows and deepens in complexity, taking along with it the winds of an ever rising storm and persecuting rain.

The times dwindle and lessen as we seek His face. Time on earth will fade to an eventual close, but the rejoicing and reigning with our King, Jesus Christ, will be everlasting and wonderful. But those wonderful days ahead will only be for the ones strong enough to withstand this great storm that is now upon us. **Be prepared.** Put on the armor of God, because although the war has been ongoing since the beginning of time, the battles we face are straight ahead. Unfortunately some will perish. We must always be rooted in good soil, empty of the world, and ready to be filled with the righteousness of God to live in accordance to

His plan. Nothing else. All who continue without the strength of Jesus will falter and fail, but with His help we will be victorious and dwell in the presence of our ever-loving Father.

I search the sky for answers to the coming days, but the storm will bring all of the answers I seek. I know that God has put me here for the purpose of warning His followers of the times ahead. Rejoice even at the pinnacle of darkness and let the love of God light your path and lead you into His kingdom. Seek Him, and you shall find all the answers to everything your heart desires to know. Relinquish all hate and love what He has created. Keep your heart strong and true, because the love of God has lengthened your life and rendered you hope. Believe in the words I say, because they are from Him and for His glorification. Lift up His name and rejoice in all He has done for you. Be thankful and continue in His works. Sail on in the voyage to be closer to Him. Remain a holy vessel. Open up, and pour His love back upon the earth. The days are growing shorter so make each moment count by following the conviction of the Holy Spirit as He moves within you. Believe in me as I believe in you. Together in Christ's name we are bound by His love and work through His grace. Rejoice and proclaim His power and wonderful presence in your life.

Sunshine in the Rain

Weary and distressed, I long for the comfort my Almighty God offers freely to those who seek His face. I love my God so much, and He shows us time and again exactly how much more

He loves us though we fail Him daily. I voyage on not knowing how the Lord will work through me in the coming days, but I rejoice in that although the rain of evil is falling and corruption is in the midst, God Almighty reigns. He will continue to work in all of His children according to His purpose, and not once should we question His authority. Abide in Him through faith and love. God is a just God and His rule stands forever. No matter what passes away and the seasons bring, the Lord Almighty will be our Savior and King. Jesus lives! Praise God! Not once does He turn from us or leave us by ourselves, but in all things He grants mercy and gives hope and strength to the lost and weary. He is a light in the darkness and a beacon for the lost.

The world is growing in despair, and the years are bringing with the times storms and great chaos. But in these tough times we must seek God more than ever. Pray for our communities and cities. Pray for others in need around the globe. The heavens will shake and the earth will rumble! Bind us together, oh God! Many are persecuted, broken, and betrayed today around the world! Lift up your voices in one cry, and ask God to see us through this great peril!

We must seek Him at once—turn back—and the worries of this world will dissipate and fade, for we know that God in Heaven is ruler on earth and in the skies above. He will forever dwell with His followers. We should follow those convictions of the heart and accept Him as Lord and Savior, because His ways are perfect and true.

As the winds breathe in the corruption and evil that saturates a hate-filled world, they battle against the love and devotion of God which manifests strength in all His children. All will come to feel the almighty power of the Lord, and many will be turned from their wicked ways. The coming storm will wreak havoc upon the world in incomprehensible ways, but those who remain and abide in Christ shall make it through to the coming sun. Then His children shall be taken and the wrath of God will fall upon the land and spread throughout the earth.

Though the nights will be dark and the winds strong, seek the Son of God. Allow Him to manifest His powerful light in your life in the midst of utter chaos and perilous darkness. Look to the living King as your confidant when all others fail you. Let Him be the sunshine during the dreary, rainy nights when a knock at the door is so close to being heard. Listen to His call.

The earth quakes and the heavens roar at the almighty power of the Living God. Believe in His promises, and He will give you a cloud of refuge during the day and a pillar of fire in your heart by night through a storm so undeniably strong and vicious (Nehemiah 9:12). The sole purpose of the battles ahead are to redeem the name of the Lord Almighty and bring His church back to unified purity. All that follows are the effects of the vicious attack from Satan's jealousy, and the darkness will rage against all believers amidst an unparalleled storm. Holy and consuming will the love of God encompass His followers, shielding them from the devastation, and they will take refuge in the power of the Almighty God.

I praise and worship You, oh Lord, for Your divine blessings and the power of Your holy presence given in this great time of despair. Shed light into our lives so darkness might not overcome us. Give us strength to persevere with the hope and sunshine from within. Give us mercy, oh God, so the peak of this storm might be spared from us in our time. Save us Jesus. Send out Your divine Spirit through the storm to catch and rescue the unbelieving fleers. Keep us in the eye of the storm Lord, until that time when you shall ride the clouds of the sky into the storm and save us from the disasters ahead.

Reveal Your mighty wonders among those who do not believe so they may know Your power, oh Lord. Keep us close so we might not stray and allow the storm to catch us. Watch over us and be our light in the darkness of the night. Be our sunshine in the rain so that Your holy promise may be seen to all who believe and know that Your mercy, oh Lord, is forever. To those who seek You, let them be guided into the works of Your awesome will, oh God. Bind up those who follow You and keep them close to You. Work in those who desperately seek Your face, so they may know their faith has made them whole. Find all who long to be in Your holy presence and do Your will in them Jesus. Transform hearts and minds so they may walk in Your sight and find favor in Your eyes. Lead them down the narrow road of righteousness, and lend Your divine hand unto them, so they may worship You and have the strength to do Your perfect will in such harsh temptations.

I find my strength in You, oh God, and I come to You with my troubles. You are my fortress and my shelter. The storm will not penetrate, but the barricade of Your love will block the evil and hate spewing from its deceptive leader. Bring judgment Jesus, so he may know You are the Living God. Let no one find comfort but through Your name. Let Your grace be my guide and shield us with Your divine presence and power. Dress us in Your holy armor Jesus, so that we might endure all temptation and corruption and not fall into the pit of deceit and maliciousness.

The world has and will continue to see pain and turmoil of an unbearable nature. The day of the Lord is close at hand and who shall survive it? Be ready so you may avoid that terrible time! Be ready so that you might be spared from that great day of disaster.

Give your whole being to God. Lie upon the altar of the Lord and just let it all go. Prepare your hearts and minds for the battles ahead, for they are not for the frail of mind or the weak at heart. Our faith in Him should lift us up and keep us through the rains. These are sunny days compared to what lies ahead. Be spared from the disaster, and seek refuge in your Lord. Carry Him with you at all times so your soul will be allowed to inherit what is rightfully yours. Believe that He is coming for you, and the rest will just be wind going by on a cloudy day. The storm will be long and grueling, but we are given hope in a glorious destiny of truth. His Word shall keep us in all situations, and we shall know the glory of the Living God.

The Bible, words of truth sent from God to man so your soul might be edified in Him, unlocks the mysteries to godly understanding. Long to know more about Him and His love. You can never be close enough to God. Always seek a closer walk with Jesus. A holy walk it is and He loves you from the very last ounce of His being. Rejoice in the name of God. Allow Him to work in you the way a father teaches a son or daughter about life. Seek light and truth in darkness and deception so your refuge may be in peace and harmony until the hour of the unknown comes.

The time of the end approaches. Very soon shall it be indeed, but as it is written we shall only know the season in which He comes. The day and hour are unknown, but God alone knows when we shall be saved from the storm. The storm will bring the gateway to His coming. Open your eyes and see the power of God on Earth and in your life. Allow Him to use you according to His perfect plans for your life, and you shall grow stronger day by day. Vow to yourself to be steadfast and loyal to His teachings and commandments so your closer walk with Him may bring heavenly rewards. My faith lives in the comfort of His arms in a strong desire to draw closer to Him. Belong in the holy army of God and go to war against the darkness of this world! Separate yourselves!

Shed sunshine on the earth while rain is pouring on your head. The Lord seeks to comfort you and all those nearby. Let His love overflow throughout your soul so others might taste of His mighty power and divine presence. Feed your soul. Embrace these truths, and follow your heart, sanctified by the Spirit of God. Seek the light of the sun in a dreary night yet to come. Fellow brothers and sisters in Christ, be prepared for the day and hour are but a mystery yet to be revealed. Follow the path provided, and have faith you will emerge victorious in Christ's name.

Glorious Presence

As the winds blow by, my holy vessel becomes secluded, holy, and untouched by the opposing winds and futile storms. God has revealed in me power unknown by men lacking an understanding heart, but those in the refuge of God are justified in the Lord's incredible power. I worship and glorify His name throughout the earth. I relish in His holy, divine blessings, and I thankfully seek more from Him each and every day. I long to be pleasing in His sight, and the day must come when we realize that God's power is among us always, through even the darkest of afflictions.

The glory of God is powerful, and those who are afflicted by the enemy and are persecuted for His sake must take comfort that His impending wrath is coming upon the world. **"Your justice will come,"** says God. Many will encounter His wrath in the years ahead, but in the meantime you, who are called by His name, **must**, and I mean ***must***, step up and accept what is expected from you. We each have a calling from the Lord, but only those who seek the face of God and walk forward in their calling, appointed by God Himself, will truly be blessed for their work. The mysterious ways in which God moves teaches us to walk by faith and not by sight, for we do not know the new mission called upon us in the mornings after our greatest battles.

Be ever vigilant and ready warriors of God. Rest easy in His name during the late night hours, for we are to go to work with the rising sun. Take His strength, and carry it forth into the darkness. His presence keeps you safe from harm. I take each day as one whole but to a larger part of something far greater, and I seek His face without ceasing in prayer and passionate worship. He continues to bless those obedient to His voice and ready to sacrifice their mortal flesh for the glory of God. Lay yourselves upon the altar and sacrifice your bodies for His kingdom's sake. Fill the throne room of God with new souls won into His army. Strengthen the numbers, one by one, and know He has filled us with His ever-powerful manifest glory.

God's presence has been misunderstood for a long time. Many people become satisfied with His anointing power while they are singing and rejoicing in worship but do not realize that the power of His Holy Spirit can take you and keep you all parts of the day. His Spirit protects and guides you. His Spirit keeps you in the blackest of night when the flame of God burns brightest into the darkness. Do not let the dread of peril and persecutions weaken your resolve. Eternal glory awaits in Heaven for your sacrifice. Hold nothing back. Reserve nothing for yourself. Fill your soul with faith and your mouths with the words of His anointing. His Spirit leads you home and to the darkest corners of a loveless world. Put your faith in Him, and

His Holy Spirit will show you the path to travel. Shine your light, and His Spirit will strengthen your resolve to make it through the night. Lie down and forget about your cares of the world, because He feeds you with the eternal bread of life. Eat and be filled.

Worshiping the Lord our God gives our spirit within us satisfaction, because we know He is pleased with our obedience. God's glory is everlasting, and He longs to fill a searching heart found empty from troubled times and overwhelming despair.

Sometimes those who are the called are appointed to their time and place by God, and we are sent out into the world whether ready or not. He pulls you in, and you must face Him. He eats at your worldly resolve and His Spirit lifts you up from these troubled times and gives you the gifts and tools you need to fight the battles ahead. Accept your calling, step forward, and be battle ready, for the time is now.

Paul tells us in 1 Thessalonians 5:19 to, **"Quench not the Spirit."** To emphasize, the Holy Trinity consists of three divine members with unique and quite distinguishingly different personalities and characteristics. One part of God is the Holy Spirit, and He is the Helper and most sensitive of the three. Jesus bluntly states in Matthew 12:31, **"Wherefore I say unto you, all manner of sin and blasphemy shall be forgiven unto men: but the blasphemy against the Holy Ghost shall not be forgiven unto men. And whosoever speaketh a word against the Son of man, it shall be forgiven him: but whosoever speaketh a**

word against the Holy Ghost, it shall not be forgiven him, neither in this world, neither in the world to come" (KJV).

I do not believe people understand the depth of hurt Jesus Christ feels when those reserved for His love do not accept Him, but instead choose to live in the cares and worries of the world. To sacrifice His body so completely and to fulfill throughout His entire life every expectation God the Father had for Him without error, He died for us and gave us the easiest choice we could ever make. He paid the price because no one else could! How far God would go to guarantee your eternal soul, and yet many choose instead to pursue passions and lusts of the flesh and embrace the darkness of this temporary world! How dangerous this world has become.

Through our self-seeking hearts, we have abandoned even in the body of Christ the gifts and workings of the Holy Spirit. Through repentance and release of pride and self we can once again capture the zest and personality of God within our lands. We must turn fully from the world and fall on our faces before a gracious and merciful God. Weep between the porch and the altar, oh adulterous nation! For you have been found guilty of worshiping other Gods and living in the ways of the world. Forsake your idols and commit yourselves to the glory of God's kingdom! *There is no other way.*

How long are we going to keep our eyes open and our hearts closed? Have you ever gone to church on a Sunday morning looking for something miraculous to happen? Did you get there and hope to witness God's power filled throughout your soul and that He would manifest throughout the entire church? This is God's desire. He wants our faith in Him to increase so that we do not just believe, but instead ***know*** His Spirit will bring power and great glory. The power of His blood and the anointing on those He chooses will usher in the promises of His Word. If we are to believe, then we are to live accordingly. Do not cast your doubts upon the sick, but instead place your faith in Jesus Christ. His purpose prevails. Our job in this life is to praise Him and to live by His teachings. We are to take that Word and deliver His message to the doorsteps of every home and to the narrow corners of the globe. When will you step down from the dividing line and join the Army of God?

Now is the time.

"**Come**," says the Lord. "**Come, and I will make you fishers of men**," (Matthew 4:19).

You cannot go to church, live in the light, shine the light, be in the Spirit of God, and yet still have fun in the world with your unbelieving friends. You will not see the glory of God living that kind of life. God is a just God. Nothing impure and unholy will inherit the kingdom of God. **"On that day, many will say to me, 'Lord, Lord, did we not prophesy in your name, and cast out demons in your name, and do many mighty works in your name?' And then will I declare to them, 'I never knew you; depart from me, you workers of lawlessness'"** (Matthew 7:22-23 ESV).

Eternally gracious and divine is our Lord Jesus, and He died so we might live, even with our flaws and sinful nature. He loved us so very much that His blood was shed from the cross to

His grave because of our iniquities. How foolish we have become and sedentary in our lives of sin! Repent before God, and become desperate for the Lord. Seek His face and turn your lives over to Him before the time draws too late.

Begin to understand that God's endless mercy and divine righteousness cannot be taken for granted or used selfishly. He does not want to see what you can do for Him but wants to see how much you are willing to give up so that He can do for you and through you. Examine your heart. Does it sincerely reflect the teachings of God and yearn for the filling of His Holy Spirit? If it does then we are on our way.

Pray to Him at this very moment. Close your eyes, and seek His face. Search for Him. *Really **search** for Him.* He will bring you His sanctifying Spirit upon you in such wondrous power that I myself am feeling His divine presence as I write this. In faith I am asking God to touch you now and make it so. Rejoice! For God will do for you if you seek Him and ask in prayer through a trembling, desperate heart.

Asking is the key to receiving. Have faith that your prayer will be heard, and you will be sanctified and filled, and your cup shall run over in abundance. David, the great king of Israel, writes in Psalms 23 that God anoints our head with oil and makes our cup to run over. God fills us with His holy and divine presence so we may get a taste of eternal glory and know He is God forever. Look toward the heavens and seek the power of God. Just as the sun in midday heat blinds the senses, let the power of God blind us from the temptations of the world. Look at the face of God's endless love and mercy so we might be blinded from all sin and led down the road of righteousness.

Do not try to walk the dark road alone weary traveler. Allow God Almighty to lead you into a newfound and blossoming relationship so that one day we can look through trained eyes and no longer worry about falling into the deceit of the world. In that time the world will have perished in its corruption and God's wrath will have sufficed over all evil. Then we may reign with Jesus and know we are truly His. The Lord loves us all, and He is coming soon. God Almighty only knows the day and hour, but He allows us to know the season. We are in the opening moments of events the world shall not survive. Look at His promises and the prophecy shown unto His willing servants, the prophets, and know the time is drawing near.

Set your eyes upon the throne room of God and do not stop praying until you are trained and equipped with all the necessities for battle. Pray and meditate on God's Word. Rise up from the ashes, and live in the Spirit with the anointing from an Almighty God.

Allow Him to work in and through you. Our only limitations are those set by worldly minds rooted in the sins of this earth. Root your mind in the Word, and you will know the full extent of God's power. Destroy the walls and the boundaries between your hearts and minds and the will of God. Know that God is all-powerful and passionate about His children. He made us in His image, and by His love we received grace.

Where have you placed your expectations? God will reveal in you a mission and a plan. ***Seek Him with a desperate heart.*** Ask Him for a willingness to go anywhere to witness and preach His Word.

I love Him with my whole heart and know my Jesus will have mercy on anyone who cries out to Him. Look to Him for the love you need. Search for His glorious presence and rejoice, because He has offered you an opportunity to do something great here in the last days. From the words of Revelation 22:12, Jesus says, **"And, behold, I come quickly; and my reward is with me, to give every man according as his work shall be"** (KJV). His promises endure. Remember Jesus lived a sinless life and is the son of God. The rewards will come to those who do as the Lord says and follow the calling given them.

His love abounds, and His presence is magnified through us all. Live each day in sight of what must be done. I continue in this voyage with God to become closer to Him every passing hour of the day. I render my heart to Him and have kept nothing back. I have been faithful to the call of the Holy Spirit and shall follow with faith and dedication. Let His promises ring true in my soul! He leads me into the path of righteousness for His name's sake. Follow Him, and He will shed light upon your path and hope into your heart. Rejoice in Jesus' name.

I love You Jesus.

Precious Gems

Pursuing the fruit of the Spirit, the future holds in store for me blessings unknown and not yet fully understood. Longing for the Word of God, I chase after an essence of Him of which I have not seen but only felt. Like the breeze against my face, my God's power cleanses and cools my soul from the harmful rays of the world's scorching sun. Oh that You would enlarge my coast Jesus, that I might work in Your name. Let Your glory be poured upon my head and Your anointing power saturate Your work in me and through me. Be gentle in molding Your children, but let the fruit of Your labor working through us be powerful and forever bring glory to Your name, oh God.

Oh that Your hand would be with me Jesus in all I do, so that I might glorify your precious name in every word and deed. Use me according to Your plans for my life, oh God, so that I might be obedient and a favorable sight in Your eyes. Glorify Yourself through me as a living testimony of Your love, oh Lord. Let Your name resound in my ears even at the pinnacle of darkness. Protect me in Your mighty arms, oh Father, and rescue me from my enemies. Keep me from evil that I may not cause pain to others. Pour out upon me all of Your power and glory. Make my cup to overflow so that all who come near might find conviction through Your wonderful Spirit—that they might be saved from their sinful ways and made holy in Your eyes.

Live through me in every word and deed so others will find strength in my example. Lead me down the path toward true holiness in Your name. Work through me like You worked through Moses. Help me to find a soft spot in Your heart like David. Give me the wisdom of Solomon and the faith of Elijah and Elisha. Help me to trust in Your plan like Daniel trusted You, oh God, and to understand Your plan is much bigger than just me. Help me to work courageously in the faith and to be bold in the Spirit like Peter. Teach me to have the knowledge of Paul, the prophetic gifts of John, and the righteousness of You, Jesus.

Bring me along in this voyage of holiness and peace, and guide me into Your loving blessings and gracious giving, so I might be molded in the form of Your apostles from long ago. Hear my prayer, oh Lord. My plea has been brought before You, and I continue in faith toward Your response. Only for You do I work. For Your name's sake do I venture on not knowing what tomorrow brings but with faith anticipating the workings of Your divine glory and loving Spirit. Let the stars of the night sky be as just a glimmer of the vast array of glory You shall display through us and in us in these last days, Father. The love You have for us demonstrates the quality of beauty and depth that not even the most precious gems can compare.

Spiritual gifts sparkle and dance like diamonds across the coastline, deposited along the shore from the crashing waves of God's Holy Spirit. Follow the precious gems God has provided in your life so you might grow and learn in the Spirit and become a part of God's plan for this world. He has sounded the call for battle and let out a resounding battle cry for young warriors to be trained up for such a time as this. The time is nigh. The danger lurks, and evil runs rampant around you. He has called you into war for a reason. You have a purpose with God. **No one else can do it. God has called *you*.**

Shed light into the dark crevices of Satan's corruption. Stand firm in the faith, and be steadfast in the truth, always sticking close to the Word of God. Don't be content with where you are now but venture forward knowing one day this long and grueling battle of a walk with Jesus against all evil will get you to the glorious doorstep beyond Heaven's pearly gates. Then you will know that you are precious gems to the Lord, and He keeps you near to His heart always.

Seek to be at His side at all times so you can know He is directing your every move. Believe in Him to work through you so that you might not become boastful or arrogant of your relationship with Him but loving and nurturing to those who are in need of the Lord's love. Allow Him to guide you in every moment, not allowing others to bring down His name or to kill your faith.

Do not look back at a world to be forgotten, for the ways of Sodom are destruction and gloom. Stare straight, and put your eyes upon the Lord. He will guide your paths, even if to the mountains in the wilderness. Trust His plan for you, and listen when the Spirit of God speaks. Obey His voice, for we do not always understand the ways of the Lord. He moves mysteriously through us, and our obedience is crucial to His plans. Understand this war is bigger than us and is taking place in the heavens. Listen and obey.

Our Father in Heaven cherishes each of His children. The world will pass away, but the believing, righteous souls shall live eternally with Him. That's why when we love the ways of the world and forget the sacrifice He made for us at the cross, we undermine the ways of God and discredit Him. Do not burden God's heart with foolish pursuits and childish meanderings. When we walk away from God, we show our love for the temporary has sufficed over our love for the everlasting.

Precious as we are to God, sometimes children of God can take for granted all He has done and become caught up in the ideas of the world. We long to be perceived as likeable and popular or possibly someone successful and with abundant fame. Does fame matter to God? One day He will return and your fame will matter as much as the dirt on the ground. What do you think is going to happen when God comes back for His people? Those in the world and unbelief will be left, and the children of God will be taken up into the clouds. The ones left will undergo God's wrath, and the ones taken will reign with Him forever.

So what then matters in the breadth of eternity if someone likes you? The measure of success in our lives will be based solely on our works in this world through the Holy Spirit. What have you done for Jesus lately? Have you ministered to the lost? Called for God's healing power to reach out to those you love and the loved ones of those around you? When is the last time you have found yourself on your knees calling out to God in surrender and supplication? Have you denounced this world and found yourself at the mercy of God's forgiveness and grace? Are you still lost in this world?

Accept His salvation, and take your prayers to the cross. Lay it down, and give it to Him today. Everything. Lay it down. Ask Him for forgiveness and for Him to come into your heart and be your Lord and Savior.

Seek His face. Seek to please God with a pure heart, and He will abundantly bless you for your efforts and save you from the doom of a sinful nature. How is it that Jesus, the Son of God, was born, lived among us, was crucified and died upon the cross at Calvary, then arose on the third day if God's love for us wasn't precious? It is more precious than tiny eyes peeking from a newborn baby for the first time. It is more precious than twinkling stars in the guiding light of the moon on a dark and beautiful night. It leads you into everlasting peace from the storm blowing in and shields you from the wrath of God which will pour from the heavens. It guides you into His work so all who have patience will glorify His name. God's love comforts us when the world is corrupted and our hearts are broken. It lifts us up so we can take another step without falling on our face. It breaks through all barriers of hate and conflict and manifests itself to those who draw near.

Worthy or not, we are put on this earth to serve God, and nothing will ever hinder me from doing just that. I have kept my eyes set upon Him so that even while the storm pours out upon the earth and conflict tears through the land, I am ready. My eyes do not drift as the ocean's waves do, but I remain steadfast in the Lord's promise to one day deliver us from all evil turmoil. My spirit grieves for those who do not find the truth in front of them but instead turn to the ways of the world and their own desires. My spirit weeps for those who know the way but are led astray for they are the ones who suffer the greatest afflictions.

Oh that You would keep me from evil that it may not grieve me, oh Lord. They know the truth and yet have fallen into reproach, failing in their duties to remain holy and pure. These precious gems have fallen from God's holy grasp and will suffer the penalty of God's future judgment. The time will come when you will stand before the judgment seat of Christ and account for all you have done. Will you be rejected by God for living in your own way and not His? Seek the truth in your heart, not turning from God's Word but keeping its truth holy and pure.

Hear the supplications of the faithful, oh God, that Your name be forever glorified among those who desperately seek You and long to take a stand for Your name's sake. Manifest Your glorious power through us all and bestow faith, so we might make it down life's narrow road. Lead us and shelter us from the storm. Guide and comfort us in the time when the wicked shall rule and hope is gone from their hearts.

Let us take refuge in Your name so all who have faith will make it until the time of Your coming. Spare us from Your wrath, oh Lord, and shield us from the destruction soon coming upon the world. I know many will be deceived, but You will have who seek You, and Your presence shall empower ... through faith in Your promises. Move in us, oh ... that You might be glorified. You are precious to me as I am ... you. Let Your hand be upon us in all that we do, oh God.

This voyage I have undertaken has led me into the realization of how important this fight is for the souls of man and the discovery of our life's true purpose. Let the love of God guide you in that relationship with Him which keeps us apart from the world and held tightly to the heart of God. Fill your soul with a passion to please Him and a desire to stay the course.

Be steadfast in the Lord. Be holy and sincere to do His will, and He will move in you as the wind blows upon the sails of a holy ship, moving it through the waters with amazing ease. Drifting in time, it knows not the destination but only the present course. The sails controlled by the mighty winds of the Spirit, He guides me into works unknown but of which I am called to perform. I desire to draw closer every day to our Lord because I know the battles ahead will test every ounce of faith we have. I believe that God will delay His return for just a little while so His children may be gathered together and drawn to His side.

Seek God and His ways will be made manifest. Follow Him and your direction will be straight and true to His course. Let Him lead you into heavenly wonder with fulfillment and joy in your heart. You are so precious in His sight. Believe you are more precious than any rare stone or gem of this earth. You are an adopted child of God and heirs and joint heirs to His eternal kingdom. Glory to God!

Word of God

Along the sky's edge, shining the light of dawn into the eyes of those who seek truth through God's Word, the mystery of the Lord is opened up and all things under Heaven are shown for your knowledge and wisdom. Leading you down the righteous road paved by men of the past, we rejoice in the power of the coming Lord. Able as the sun to shine, He brings forth glory onto the land within the prayers of the righteous.

Luscious flowers blooming in the spring, glowing with the holy scent of heavenly wonders and eternal magnificence, sway by the power of God's Spirit upon the breeze. The grass green and the leaves ripe and full of color, the Lord sheds hope into the world with His power and great glory.

Spoken through the divine utterance of God, the Word is the Lord and has been from the beginning. His hands were upon the Word as it was written, and He grips it with love and gives wisdom through it even today—*especially* today. Speaking through it He shows His direction, His purpose, and His character. The Word, the direction for getting down that road of righteousness others have paved, leads us deeper into our relationship with God, and we are on the long and grueling journey of shedding truth in times of vast darkness and convincing deception. Seek strength in the Lord through His

Word so you can make it through the trials and hardships you face in a soulless and affliction-stricken world.

Let Him lead you into the heavens with victory in your eyes, because you know with God the victory is yours to claim. There is great wonder in knowing that the Lord is so gracious to each of us. We love Him, but He loves us so much more. His eyes are soft and warm with love and devotion, desiring to always be passionate to those who look to the Word in their quest to be closer to Him and for His will to be accomplished in their lives.

He leads you down a path through the dangers of this world, but the barrier of His love guards and protects you from evil. The torch of Christ lights your path as danger lurks in the shadows. His light guides and keeps you safe so His purposes can be completed. I pray you sincerely seek Him. Let His will be done in your life so He can work in and through you effectively. Humble yourselves unto the Lord and go forth with humility in your heart and joy throughout your soul.

Live for God, and He will manifest His plans for you. Deny yourselves the offerings of the world. They are temporary and fleeting, empty and without sustenance. But the Spirit of God revives you daily, allowing your hardest day to find the grip upon the path toward tomorrow's trek forward. Be strong in the faith, and seek the Lord wholeheartedly.

The days are short, and the warnings are upon the signs of the clouds. Pack up your belongings and move from the world of desire, lustful sin, and unholy corruption and move to the loving, abiding shelter of God and His amazing grace. He proves

His love for us daily and our lives serve as beautiful examples. Look at what you have. Genuinely see what God has provided for your house and family. Everything the Lord has given comes from Him, and He asks that you give it back in the form of total denial of self and servitude toward others, with brotherly love and dedicated outward profession of His sacrifice for us. Understand God provides when we have total faith in His complete control in every facet of our lives.

When we have denied self, He works through us to spread His glory unto the world so all may know the glorious promise of His salvation, provided to all who believe in Jesus Christ and profess His name as Lord over their lives. When we come to God having denied self and focused only on His guidance, we please Him. When we set our eyes upon obedience to Him and cast aside the pleasures of the world, we find His favor.

Make yourself available to the hands of God as a willing vessel, empty of all impurities of evil thoughts, sexual immorality, theft, murder, adultery, coveting, wickedness, deceit, sensuality, envy, slander, and pride (Mark 7:21-22). He will purify you in His Holy Spirit and pour out His abundance and glory so you can go into a corrupted world with the power of healing and great deliverance for those under the illumination of God's light.

The Word of God is the movement and direction of the Spirit. What the Word shows, the Spirit obeys through His command when we act in willingness. When light breaks forth into the windows of our houses in early morning, it forewarns the coming of the sun. Surely God's Word is the direction of the Spirit put here for us to see and understand the ways of God and the mysteries in which He works. Though some of you may not always welcome the direction the Holy Spirit is moving you, you continue to wonder why God uses others in such significant ways. Be willing and obedient to His voice and the words upon your heart. See the direction God wants you to travel, and be sure of your plan before you depart. Rely on Him and nothing can stop you—not even death of mortal flesh.

Our sinful natures keep us from abundant blessings, because even though our sins are forgiven, any willful habitual sins separate us from the favor of God. We need to pray we turn from those ways and for strength in Him to not return. In 2 Chronicles 7:14 it says, **"If my people, which are called by my name, shall humble themselves, and pray, and seek my face, and turn from their wicked ways, then I will hear from heaven and forgive their sin and heal their land"** (KJV). Brothers and sisters, until the Church does this, the glory of God cannot be revealed, plain and simple. The time has come for total surrender. Place yourselves in the perfect will of God and be a part of the greatest outpouring in the history of the world. Watch as He pours out His spirit upon all flesh! May the world tremble at the feet of God's great power and glory!

As it says in Joel 2:28, **"And it shall come to pass afterward, that I will pour out my spirit upon all flesh; and your sons and your daughters shall prophesy, your old men shall dream dreams, your young men shall see visions"** (KJV). God didn't say He would work in just adults who have known Jesus for years, but it says His spirit will be poured out upon all flesh, whether young or old, big or small. Since the early church this prophecy has been being fulfilled, and in the present time His Spirit has continued to move among His faithful.

Joel 3:9 says, **"Proclaim ye this among the Gentiles; Prepare war, wake up the mighty men, let all the men of war draw near; let them come up"** (KJV). The Lord has shown that these are days in which we need to wake up the mighty warriors of God and pray without ceasing and fight for His cause. We are to draw near to God and give Him the necessary authority over every resource from within us so He may work through us as the instruments of His will and workings.

The success of our country's revival in the Spirit of God hinges upon the body of Christ being obedient to His commands. Give God full control. If you trust Him as you are called to trust Him then give Him full control over your life. Full control. We need to come up from the world of bitter deceit, lay out the mighty will of God before all of the warriors of God's army, and prepare for spiritual battle. The darkness has manifested in this world, and Christians are being persecuted and killed daily.

"Now is the time! Let them come up!" says God.

Seek strength in the Lord through the edifying power of the Holy Spirit, for it is written in Joel 2:26, **"And ye shall eat in plenty, and be satisfied, and praise the name of the Lord your God, that hath dealt wondrously with you: and my people shall never be ashamed"** (KJV). You can eat plentifully and be satisfied with the strengthening power of the Holy Spirit, and rejoice in the name of God for He has worked mightily in you. You will forever be thankful for His blessings and never be ashamed.

Let the Spirit of God guide you into His workings so you can rejoice in the name of the Lord and know you are doing it not through your own will or might but by His will and calling. You can be joyful for it is written to make a joyful noise (Psalm 100:1) and know that God Almighty is with you in everything you do, and His comfort and love dwells in you, bringing forth strength every day. God spoke to the Israelites in Amos 5:4 saying "**Seek ye me, and ye shall live**" (KJV). He asks the same of us today.

The Word of the Lord stands forever, and He makes it so clear that we are blessed among the nations. Live by His words, and seek truth and understanding as to what God is bringing upon the world. In Psalms 74:3 (KJV) it says, **"For I was envious at the foolish, when I saw the prosperity of the wicked."** God has rung the bell for His mighty warriors to wake up from their slumber like His disciples once slept in the Garden of Gethsemane, because we are on the brink of war. We shall fight for our Lord and Savior, Jesus Christ. In Psalms 74:18 (KJV), it says **"Surely thou didst set them in slippery places: thou castedst them down into destruction."** And in verse 23, **"Nevertheless I am continually with thee: thou hast holden me by my right hand."**

Jesus is a loving, merciful God, and we must come to realize that He is in control. Over everything we do, He is in control. He will pour out His Spirit on all flesh as the prophet Joel states, and as it says in Psalms 74:10, **"Therefore his people return hither: and waters of a full cup are wrung out to them"** (KJV). God is calling His people back to Him. **"All who once knew Me and have turned away, come back,"** says the Lord.

I love Him so very much. Now is the time when you should discern your love. Which is more important—your love for an everlasting God who shows mercy and lives by His Word, whose promises never stand broken, or do you live for a world which will one day come to an end and all therein be condemned for the evil committed? It says in Psalms 75:10, **"All the horn of the wicked also will I cut off; but the horn of the righteous shall be exalted"** (KJV).

The Lord is a powerful God to be feared and who seeks justice for the afflicted. Let Him be the ruler of your life. Turn from your wicked ways and know the God of Abraham, Isaac, Jacob, and the holy covenant in which they have carried will stand for the covenant brought upon you as a holy member of God's army. It says in Revelation that the time is coming, and the mystery of God will be accomplished. It clearly states in Revelation 22:12, **"And, behold, I come quickly; and my reward is with me, to give every man according as his work shall be"** (KJV).

The Lord has also invites the thirsty to taste of His holy, filling waters in Revelation 22:17 saying, **"And the Spirit and bride say, Come. And let him that heareth say, Come. And let him that is athirst come. And whosoever will, let him take the** water of life freely" (KJV). Clearly the Word of God Almighty promises spiritual fulfillment through the Holy Spirit.

"Come," says the Lord.

The Word of the Lord God in Revelation 10:6-7 (KJV) says, "**And sware by him that liveth for ever and ever, who created heaven, and the things that therein are, and the earth, and the things that therein are, and the sea, and the things which are therein, that there should be time no longer: but in the days of the voice of the seventh angel, when he shall begin to sound, the mystery of God should be finished, as he hath declared to his servants the prophets.**"

The One True God in Heaven and the Lord who rules the universe has a message we need to hear. We need to bring our lives and love back to Him in the fully committed manner of which we are called.

The Word says in Psalms 77:13-20 (KJV):

> "**Thy way, O God, is in the sanctuary: who is so great a God as our God? Thou art the God that doest wonders: thou hast declared thy strength among the people. Thou hast with thine arm redeemed thy people, the sons of Jacob and Joseph. Selah.**
>
> "**The waters saw thee, O God, the waters saw thee; they were afraid: the depths also were troubled. The clouds poured out water: the skies sent out a sound: thine arrows also went abroad. The voice of thy thunder was in

the heaven: the lightnings lightened the world: the earth trembled and shook.

"Thy way is in the sea, and thy path is in the great waters, and thy footsteps are not known. Thou leddest thy people like a flock by the hand of Moses and Aaron."

Let God lead you into the Promised Land by being obedient to His commands, destroying any idols in your lives, and following His voice wherever it may lead you..

Show us, oh God. I worship Your holy name. Glory be to You, oh Savior and Redeemer. Show us Your power and glory and fill us with Your Spirit. I love You, oh Lord. Visit us and show us Your manifest glory. Lend Your hand to us and show us Your face, oh God.

I see the times drawing near. Draw near to God's love so you may be afforded shelter from the storm and can continue in this ever-manifesting voyage with our Lord and Savior. God is a mighty God. Truly He will overcome the terror and see us through the storm so our ship may prevail and our lives may be spared and live eternally with Him in His holy presence. The angels sing the coming of the Lord.

Signs of the Times

Shielding all that the winds produce while emanating from the innermost portions of our spirits, the holy and powerful workings of the Holy Spirit move and comfort the open and seeking hearts which long for restoration. Those willing vessels which seek God and desire correction and chastening for sinful faults—so His heavenly presence can be stronger in our lives—keep us in His favor and perfect will. He treasures our loyalty and willful submission. His love comforts us so the days coming will be shielded from us, and our hope will be forever kept in the center of our hearts because God is hope.

The times to come shield the blind from the heart of God, but the believers in Christ—trusting in His every word and leaning not into their own understanding but live through faith in Christ—shall be eternally rewarded.

The storm is blowing in with the fierce strength of a mighty giant, and the only shield we have is our faith in Christ Jesus. Like little David, we shall call upon God as our fortress and refuge. He keeps us in the five-fold ministry of which Paul outlined in his epistle to the Ephesians.

Paul wrote that the Lord "**gave the apostles, the prophets, the evangelists, the shepherds and teachers, to equip the saints for the work of the ministry, for building up the body of Christ, until we all attain to the unity of the faith and of the knowledge of the Sons of God, to mature manhood, to the measure of the stature of the fullness of Christ, so that we may no longer be children, tossed to and fro by the waves and carried about by every wind of doctrine, by human cunning, by craftiness in deceitful schemes. Rather, speaking the truth in love, we are to grow up in every way into him who is the head, into Christ, from whom the whole body, joined and held together by every joint with which it is equipped, when each part is working properly,** makes the body grow so that it builds itself up in love" (Ephesians 4:11-16 KJV).

Our callings begin with a time of preparation and end in being appointed for the work and commissioned and released toward the completion of His purpose. Take your time of preparation seriously. Seek God with a whole heart and press in to Him so you are rooted firmly in good soil. Build your house upon the Rock, and His Spirit will prepare you for all things. The Spirit of God should control our actions and guide us forward into the ministry so we can be successful in glorifying His name through obedience and fervency of heart.

Should not God's Word be meditated upon night and day, believing all that is in the holy book? Still some refuse to believe the prophecies of His servants, and they shun His warnings and teachings. The Lord says, "**Surely after my wrath has passed before you upon the earth, you will know that the Lord God reigns eternally.**" Should we blame God for His wrath and judgment upon the world, or should we take responsibility for the world's actions upon ourselves realizing that the Lord is bringing fire to a nation of unbelievers and a world of growing evil. We have largely failed those lost souls around us while we complacently allowed the church system to become tarnished and corrupt.

The times are showing themselves one by one, and all should heed to the prophets' warnings of God's judgment. All will be revealed which has not been forgiven. The Lord God knows what the darkness holds in the blackened hours of the night. The wrath of His judgment will come to those who are spiritually unready. He will show His power and glory and redeem His name to those who stomp upon it as the swine plow the mud. He will show His glory in heaven and upon the earth, and all will know that He is Lord.

In the end those who have been judged and remain will call upon the name of the Lord only to be sadly redirected to the path they had once chosen. But then after the judgment has been set, they are abandoned only to find the times from the dropping sands of chance have faded and vanished and left only torment and wrath. For surely the men rejecting the words of God's love deserve His judgment in the lake of fire. No one shall avoid His judgments and penalties, because the Lord God rules forever. His words stand to all. Redemption or condemnation.

Let us turn from our wicked ways and sway not into evil's sin and corrupted path; let the fountains of God's Holy Spirit revive us internally, and our spirit will glow of His translucent power and glory without tarnishing His promises to one day deliver from His wrath and dwell with us as heirs to the kingdom of God.

The Lord warns us:

"The ways of the Lord have been shown to you, and I will show you a new thing in Heaven and on earth, and it shall be as the days of Noah when the sons of man and the sons of God shall cast down their lots upon the earth, and all things shall be quickened. In this time I will show My power and great glory upon the earth, and

you shall know that the day of the Lord draws near. In these things you shall see signs and wonders untold such as the world has never seen. My glory approaches you even now for the world has turned against Me and was once a holy and fearful nation but now resolves itself in the pits and abyss of Hell, the scum of all things that were once holy.

"These things shall be shown to you for you to see and for the world to feel and know, and in this time you shall know that I am the one true God, and these things shall come to pass, for the great and terrible day of the Lord approaches and is here even now as the winds begin to swiftly follow its course into the world."

The times are bringing with them increased evil, and the storm will show its power in the physical and spiritual realms. All who know the Word of the Lord will be revived and reformed into the proper and holy body of Christ, and all that continue afterward to shield themselves from His love will not know that the day of Jesus's coming will have passed and the door for His wrath opened to pour upon the earth. The words of the Lord say that wickedness shall increase, but the righteous will draw nigh, enveloped by the love of His Spirit and powerful arms of restful solitude.

Do not let the words of the Lord pass you by without you giving Him complete authority over your life. He shields our souls from wickedness and cleanses us through His manifest Spirit. He holds our hearts and loves us with tender devotion.

Let the love of God guide you into the meaningful relationship granted to the believer in salvation through the blood of Jesus Christ. Open, and all shall be poured into. Turn back, and all shall be redeemed. **"Seek My face,"** says the Lord, **"and I will make you as the prophets of long before."** His people shall be redeemed and turned away from the ways of worldly manifestations, and His Spirit will power our souls and manifest His love and Spirit throughout our entire being. Then we shall know the Lord God reigns forever and ever.

The End

Along the vast horizon of a never ending world of possibility with God—by which all things are possible—I seek to shed light into the darkness of an unbelieving world. His Word goes forth and pierces the night air, dividing asunder truth from spiritual corruption and decay, and He has given His Word to benefit those who seek Him for understanding while longing for a message. The clouds drift by, and the sky shines bright. But the coming of the end is upon us, and the future holds disaster in the lurking darkness. The end is nigh.

If uncertainties exist surrounding your relationship with Jesus Christ then please seek Him while He may be found. The Lord is coming back upon strong winds, and the clouds from the sky will rejoice in His presence with a loud roar. Please give God every single ounce of your existence in faith, dedication, and servitude. Render your heart and believe in the Son of God. Believe He came for the propitiation of our sins and reconciled us with God by His death (Romans 3:25, 5:10). The storm will be harsh, and the wrath of God awaits the unbelievers. Then His judgment shall be upon all flesh, and the lake of fire awaits those judged unworthy of the Kingdom of God.

God is bringing up His generation of warriors, and we are going to lead all who don't know Him into His love. One day the Lord will call up His followers to meet with Him in the clouds, and all of those who failed to serve Him will be left. Set your eyes upon Jesus in prayer, fasting, and worship. Read His Word and apply it to every aspect of your life. The storm will be vicious and completely unrelenting—its spiritual side something man has never experienced before.

Satan is revolting against God's love being poured out upon the earth amidst His chosen. Satan's followers are going to combat God's authority in many different ways. Be cautious so as to not be pulled in by false prophets. Read the Word so you will know the true path of righteousness and do not go astray. Let God lead you with His mighty hands into a relationship of love and heavenly blessing. Be strong and steadfast in your faith so you can be strengthened to overcome the evil schemes and devices of the enemy. Satan is powerful but with faith in God we will suffice in the end and dwell with God in His kingdom of power.

Times come and go, and the world is draining faster than ever before. The power of the Almighty God knows no limits when you walk in faith and allow His light to shine through you so as to direct your path. We stay within His perfect will, understanding that we shall all stand before the judgment seat of Christ and account for every word and deed. Ask the Lord to forgive you for your shortcomings and for the grace to overcome the temptations of this life so that you might walk in power with an expectation of the eternal rewards we shall reap in Heaven.

As the times grow ever more violent, the Word of God depicts the coming of the Lord and His impending wrath. Mark 13:6-8 says, **"And Jesus answering them began to say, 'Take heed lest any man deceive you: for many shall come in my name, saying, "I am Christ," and shall deceive many. And when ye shall hear of wars and rumors of wars, be ye not troubled for such things must needs be; but the end shall be not yet. For nation shall rise against nation and kingdom against kingdom: and there shall be earthquakes in divers places, and there shall be famines and troubles: these are the beginnings of sorrows'"** (KJV).

The Lord also warns of the storm in Luke 12:54 saying, **"And he said also to the people, 'When ye see a cloud rise out of the west, straightway ye say, "There cometh a shower," and so it is. And when ye see the south wind blow, ye say, "There will be heat," and it cometh to pass. Ye hypocrites, ye can discern the face of the sky and of the earth; but how is it that ye do not discern this time?'"** (KJV).

Why has God given us these warnings? He wants his children to be warned of the time at hand. I'm not saying we will be taken tomorrow but the days are drawing near. It says in John 3:5-6 (KJV), **"Jesus answered, 'Verily, verily, I say unto** thee, except a man be born of water and of the Spirit, he cannot enter into the kingdom of God. That which is born of the flesh is flesh and that which is born of the Spirit is spirit."** Those who are born again Spirit-filled believers live by the authority of the Spiarit of God, and their faith leads them into truth and knowledge. But those who live for fleshly desires and the ways of the world will die in its corruption and one day be cast into the lake of fire. They will cry to God for entrance into Heaven, but the Lord proclaims as it says in John 7:34, **"Ye shall seek me, and shall not find me; and where I am, thither ye cannot come"** (KJV).

The Spirit of God will encompass you in the days of the end, because those who believe and are thirsty for His presence will be given their fill. We are in the days of the birth pains, and we are being revived as a body of believers by His Holy Spirit, for a great time is approaching of which the world will not escape.

But the promise of Jesus in Matthew 24:45 (KJV) says, **"Who then is a faithful and wise servant, whom his Lord hath made ruler over his household, to give them meat in due season?"** Are you the faithful and wise servant God has called you to be? If you are then you will receive your meat in due season. Seek to draw closer to God and press into Him so you can grow in the Lord and be taken from the milk.

It says in Psalms 145:14-20, **"The Lord upholdeth all that fall, and raiseth up all those that be bowed down. The eyes of all wait upon thee; and thou givest them their meat in due season. Thou openest thine hand, and satisfiest the desire of every living** thing. The Lord is righteous in all his ways and holy in all his works. The Lord is nigh unto all them that call upon him, to all that call upon him in truth. He will fulfill the desire of them that love him: but the wicked will he destroy" (KJV).

The season has come for God's glory to rain upon the earth, and we shall receive our meat in due season. Just as a new believer drinks the milk as a child would, as the believer grows, God eventually begins to feed them meat. Individually some are eating the meat, but as a body of believers, most are in many ways still drinking spiritual milk. Become a humble and willing servant for the Lord so you may be part of the coming outpouring of God's glory and spiritual harvest which sweeps across the earth. The benefits are eternal. Worship the true and living God. Storms shall rise against you, but your faith in Jesus will shield you from the fiery darts of the enemy. In the name of Jesus Christ, I ask the Lord to pour out His Spirit upon you to provide clarity and focus for the days ahead and to strengthen you and keep you vigilant.

The end is near, and the days are growing shorter. The times are growing increasingly dark, and the power of God will soon begin to manifest within the saints of God all around the world. But first we must pray and supplicate before His throne. We must usher in His presence with fervency of heart and earnestness of prayer. We must become so very desperate and come together in unity throughout the body of Christ.

Individually we need to do more. We need to press in to God every second of every day and prepare ourselves for battle.

Seek your calling and go to work for the Lord. Seek so all who do not know His wonderful love can come to know it and be saved from their transgressions and washed clean by the Holy Spirit.

My voyage to draw ever closer to the Lord and His will continues, and I live day by day in sight of all that is in store for me. As it says in Mark 16:15 (KJV), **"And he said unto them, go ye into all the world, and preach the gospel to every creature. He that believeth and is baptized shall be saved; but he that believeth not shall be damned. And these signs shall follow them that believe; in my name shall they cast out devils; they shall speak with new tongues; they shall take up serpents; and if they drink any deadly thing, it shall not hurt them; they shall lay hands on the sick, and they shall recover."**

The Word of God promises that we will perform miracles in His name if we seek His face and believe in His plan for the righteous. We will be as the apostles and prophets of long ago. The Lord gave His disciples the authority to heal the sick, raise the dead, and cause the blind to see through faith in His power if we only ask and receive with faith. Are you ready to go to work? Give God the glory and humble yourselves in repentance before the throne of God!

The end is coming, and the world is not ready. Are you? The storm will penetrate the lives of all those who are weak at heart and have understanding only in the ways of the world. Put on the whole armor of God so you can face the forces of darkness in this world with a bold face and the power of God moving through you. The Word of God, your sword of the Spirit, will cut to pieces any advance by the enemy and cause a quick retreat. Fight for His cause and allow His will to be done in your life.

Ask that your coasts be enlarged and your boundaries extended. His hand will be upon you, and He will keep you from evil, blessing you for your sacrifices. Put your trust and faith in Him. The voyage you have with the Lord Almighty is everlasting and wondrous. We will reign with Him eternally, but our responsibilities as obedient, self-sacrificing believers are to minister for Him while on earth and to serve others under God's direction. Let the end of your life on earth be the beginning of eternal life with Him. Set your sails and proclaim the glory of the coming Lord! Do not fear evil, for your faith rests in Him.

My faith is in my Lord Jesus Christ. He leads me forever into the growing depth of knowledge, wisdom, understanding, and discernment. I walk in faith that His work might always be accomplished. Have faith, for the end of the world is not yet but near. We have work to do and lives to touch. Bring others to Jesus so His name might be glorified. You will be rewarded greatly for your efforts.

The easygoing currents are behind me, and the growing waves ahead bring me into paths of the unknown, rendering work of greater depths. I long for the glory of God to overwhelm my soul but much work is at hand. I follow His heavenly wake knowing the Lord prevails, and His people shall be redeemed. Glory to the Most High God, for He lives forever and ever. Amen.

Judgment

Holy and heavenly, crashing stars from the burning desires of God pour out onto a corrupt and hate-filled world. The hate the created has for the Creator will be brought into purged judgment until the anger of the Lord has been quenched. The sheet of veiled deceit will be long forgotten, and the Almighty God shall reveal power and authority of which the souls of man could never have imagined. His anger shall rise against the idolaters of this world and no longer will He grieve for their sins. His wrath will flow forth, for His anger has come against the world and sinful humankind. He will no longer allow the blasphemy of the world against His name. He will show wonders in the heavens—blood, fire, and vapors of smoke.

He will cast the world into unknown anger and fury, and everyone shall know the Lord Almighty is ruler of all the earth. He will take vengeance against those who fanned the flames of the occult. He shall cast down the unbelievers and sentence them to eternal damnation. He shall keep the promises revealed through the words of His prophets. He will extend His fury against the beasts. No one in that day shall question the authority of God, but His power and glory will be known throughout the uttermost parts of the earth. No man or woman in that final time of increasing wrath and anger shall call upon anything but the name of Jesus Christ. Everyone will then know the full extent of God's eternal power and anger against them.

Satan will manifest himself against God, but He will fall short. The holy, heavenly King will reign forever, and we, as soldiers and followers of Jesus Christ, will no longer need our swords. Our spears will be in that time transformed into pruning hooks, and our swords shall become plowshares. No longer will pestilence and famine be among us, but the perfect love of Christ shall cover us in our holy dwelling of peace and tranquility.

The eternal damnation to those who rose against His will and led their own lives according to the desires of their hearts shall in those days see the truth in all of His glory. But they shall see from a distance. They will long for comfort and care, but only then shall they seek Him. The era of opportunity to live for God has passed them by, and they search for His love but are found wanting.

Be not deceived. These are those who in the midst of trial and tribulations denounced the name of Christ and received the Beast's mark. These are those who lived their lives according to the burning of their hearts' desires. These are those who blasphemed, cursed, and persecuted the elect of God. They shall burn forever, and His will in that time shall be complete. Those who lived for themselves or the worship of false gods shall be judged according to their deeds, and they shall be punished by the lake of burning fire and sulfur. They shall have their appearance at the Great White Throne Judgment, and His words will slice through the hope of those who will in that time seek but not find, for the times of opportunity will have vanished.

Be not deceived fellow warriors. You shall come against false prophets and be persecuted for your faith. Speak pure and true the words of Jesus Christ, exalting Him in all of His glory.

Take no thought as to the words you shall speak, but let the Spirit who manifests discernment inside you speak the Words of God before them. Walk in faith, and He will speak through you slicing with the precision of a two-edged sword. The Spirit of God will slice through the hate and corruption, and the pieces of their defenses will fall before you.

Our Lord Jesus assures us that we can truly know in our hearts and believe with abiding love that His will is being done in our lives. In 1 John 4:4 (KJV) it says, **"Ye are of God, little children, and have overcome them: because greater is He that is in you than He that is in the world."** Let the power of God manifest and run through your spiritual veins. The same way blood flows through your body, let faith course through your soul. Believe and ask in His name, and all your spiritual desires shall be granted. Jesus Christ says in John 16:23 (KJV), **"And in that day ye shall ask me nothing; verily, verily, I say unto you, whatsoever ye shall ask the Father in my name, He will give it to you."**

Be not deceived. The Lord God Almighty would not have you see these trials and tribulations, but the tares of the harvest must be weeded out and purged. We shall undergo the weeding and remain throughout the harvest. We shall be stored in the barn of God Almighty and spared from a fiery Hell and subsequent Lake of Fire. We shall not see the Harvester's wrath, but we, as useful wheat full of truth and knowledge and of good works shall be harvested and manifested under the heavenly protection of God Almighty. The truth of our deeds and glory He gives because of our willingness shall be rewarded with Crowns of Glory. He shall assemble us in the temple of His love, and we will testify the actions of our life's favor towards His will.

Let it be known and be not deceived by false doctrine. The martyred souls will be first, and the glory and honor they receive shall be praised with heavenly giving and thanks. His name shall be glorified, and the communion of His creations will at that time be shown the recognition of their deeds. The crowns granted unto us shall be eternal and everlasting. Heavenly rewards from lives of pain and persecution will be given in love and abounding glory.

He has shown you these things for the purpose of equipping you with the knowledge of truth. You shall be persecuted and there will be pain and infliction against your bodies. But God says, "**Though the world has come against you, I have been with you, and you shall see the glory of my works in full stature and power.**"

Though I leave you with words of encouragement, do not just hear with your ears but with the eyes of your heart see the truth and glory of God's work in your life. Through the power of His grace, I say unto you fellow warrior of God:

> *In the name of Jesus Christ and by the power of His love, go forth as a member of God's Holy Army. In the name of Jesus, I charge you to see through the Spirit with your heart, yet heed not the words in your ears. For the words of man are lying vanities, but the visions of the Spirit are truth and knowledge.*

From this point on in this holy voyage of God's grace, let Him completely envelop you. You will do wonders with boldness and authority, because your faith in Jesus abounds and will manifest in your life onto others. Seek God and His plans for you and have faith in His love and power. Listen to the direction and Words spoken through His Holy Spirit. Through His name and by our willingness to do His will, we will be used in ways the world has never seen. Remain humble and glorify God in all situations, for this is good unto God!

If you abide in Him and His faith abides in you, wonders untold shall prosper and spring forth from your works. Die to your mortal flesh daily as our pride is a veil to His glory. Lift up that veil and lay upon the altar. His grace is sufficient for you, for His power is perfected in your weakness (2 Corinthians 12:9). Are you ready for the voyage of a lifetime?

PART THREE
SOUNDING THE BATTLE CALL

Call To Battle

As I shift from words of encouragement and preparation, I sift through the underlying vanities. Receive these words with truth in your heart knowing they are from God alone. These messages have rendered in me a reverent fear unable to be expressed with words. I know the battles ahead are grievous and terrifying, but my heart is in it. I know I have received the call for battle from the Commander-in-Chief Himself. God Almighty has shown me in many ways I am to be on the battlefield fighting for His glory and honor, helping to save souls from destruction and rendering them unto Jesus for salvation through His blood.

The battles ahead will be harsh and pain-inflicting, but we must keep the love of God inside of us strong and manifested so that we will be able to press on during those times of trials and tribulation. In Revelation 3:8 (KJV), Jesus says to you, "**I know thy works: behold, I have set before thee an open door, and no man can shut it: for thou hast a little strength, and hast kept my word, and hast not denied my name**" (KJV). If we should continue in His name and doing His will, the world will have no authority over us. Prepare yourselves for as soon as you begin to expose the evil works of darkness, the gates of hell shall come against you. The gates of hell shall not prevail! (Matthew 16:18). They can throw us in prison, persecute us, and even kill us, but the words of God will live on.

The time has come to stop tickling people's ears and tell them the revelations the Lord presents before us. We should bring truth to the world and shed light into the darkness which fills the corrupted earth. In Revelation 3:10 (KJV), Jesus continues in saying, **"Because thou hast kept the word of my patience** [*endured in the midst of adversity*]**, I will also keep thee from the hour of temptation, which shall come upon all the world, to try them that dwell upon the earth"** (emphasis added).

But be not deceived. Only those who are holy and true and sealed with the mark of God shall be kept from the hour of temptation. The words of the Lord should engulf you at this moment as I warn you that the days ahead will require every ounce of faith you have. Press in to God throughout every hour of the day. Only those who are trained, equipped, and dressed in the full armor of God should proceed. Take all of your fears and lay them on the altar of God, because our emotions should be gone towards the battles ahead. As previously stated, we will face trials and tribulation far greater than ever before. We will be surrounded by darkness and turmoil while afflicted and in the midst of adversity. Jesus encourages in Revelation 3:12 saying, **"Him that overcometh will I make a pillar in the temple of my God, and he shall go no more out: and I will write upon him the name of my God, and the name of the city of my God, which is new Jerusalem, which cometh down out of Heaven from my God: and I will write upon him my new name"** (KJV). These things are promised by Jesus himself, so why should we doubt?

I am troubled by some who doubt the words of God even as I speak, because you shall be thrown into darkness and tried in the midst of fire. Many will perish. You will be tempted and persecuted, but the faith in you is weak without knowledge. Dress yourselves in the full armor of God.

God's armor is only effective in its entirety. Put on the breastplate of God's approval and of His righteousness so that you may be blameless and without reproach, leaving no opening for the enemy to pierce you with his fiery darts. You shall undergo intense moments of warfare against your emotions, and the darkness will seek to steal your will to fight, but the joy and peace of God shall surround you. You shall be rejected and hated for His name's sake but blessed are those who die in His name, for you shall receive Crowns of Glory. Take your shield of faith and prepare yourself for wonders and miracles untold.

Let His love guide you in each and every situation for you shall undergo adversity and only through faith will God shield us from open rejection and venomous hate. Set your eyes upon Jesus and know you will one day be rewarded for all you have accomplished for the Lord. Your efforts shall be rewarded with Crowns of Incorruptibility. Dress your feet in the shoes of preparation ready to spread the good news of salvation and peace. Keep your face on the glory of God, and you will be guided into these things with readiness and words of knowledge. The Holy Spirit of God resides in you, and you are wearing the helmet of your salvation. Know who you are in Christ and believe in His promises for your life. Dress your spirit in His love and know that you are one day going to enter into His Kingdom. The times may be troublesome and weary but let the helmet of your salvation keep you in all truth so you can persevere in the midst of these perilous times.

Dress yourselves in these, and be prepared for battle for the days ahead are unknown. Keep your sword of the Spirit which is the Word of God at the ready until the appointed time so at any moment when adversity comes upon you, you can easily overcome the temptations and trials of Satan. Fight him with the mighty words of God, and he will be defeated in his quest to tear your faith into pieces. He longs to manifest doubt inside you, but we should keep our faith during pain and affliction. If you have not patience nor perseverance seek these through prayer for they are the essentials in your weapons of warfare.

In 1 Timothy 4:1, Paul writes, **"Now the Spirit speaketh expressly, that in the latter times some shall depart from the faith, giving heed to seducing spirits, and doctrines of devils"** (KJV). We should not stray to the right or to the left but stay directly on the path ahead. **"And though the Lord give you the bread of adversity, and the water of affliction, yet shall not thy teachers be removed into a corner any more, but thine eyes shall see thy teachers: And thine ears shall hear a word behind thee saying, 'This is the way, walk ye in it, when ye turn to the right hand, and when ye turn to the left'"** (Isaiah 30:20-21 KJV).

We are being given the call to dress in the armor of God and prepare for battle. The Spirit of God shall give the glory of His presence in a magnitude never known before. But the bread of increase comes with a price. In Zechariah 13:7-9, the Lord proclaims:

"Awake, O sword, against my shepherd, against the man who stands next to me," declares the LORD of hosts. "Strike the shepherd, and the sheep will be scattered; I will turn my hand against the little ones. In the whole land, declares the LORD, two thirds shall be cut off and perish, and one third shall be left alive. And I will put this third into the fire, and refine them as one refines silver, and test them as gold is tested. They will call upon my name, and I will answer them. I will say, 'They are my people'; and they will say, 'The LORD is my God'" (Zechariah 13:7-9 ESV).

You are being prepared for the war you never knew existed. Remain in your faith and trust in these words, for they are holy and pure. I do not desire that any be slain for the faith, but I know that war renders casualties. I trust you will stand up to the responsibility of your duties:

"Gather yourselves together, yea, gather together, O nation not desired; Before the decree bring forth, before the day pass as the chaff, before the fierce anger of the Lord come upon you, before the day of the Lord's anger come upon you. Seek ye the Lord all ye meek of the earth, which have wrought his judgment; seek righteousness, seek meekness: it may be ye shall be hid in the day of the Lord's anger" (Zephaniah 2:2-3 KJV).

"Blow a trumpet in Zion; sound an alarm on my holy mountain! Let all the inhabitants of the land tremble, for the day of the LORD is coming; it is near, a day of darkness and gloom, a day of clouds and thick darkness! Like blackness there is spread upon the mountains a great and powerful people; their like has never been before, nor will be again after them through the years of all generations.

"Fire devours before them, and behind them a flame burns. The land is like the garden of Eden before them, but behind them a desolate wilderness, and nothing escapes them.

"Their appearance is like the appearance of horses, and like war horses they run. As with the rumbling of chariots, they leap on the tops of the mountains, like the crackling of a flame of fire devouring the stubble, like a powerful army drawn up for battle.

"Before them peoples are in anguish; all faces grow pale. Like warriors they charge; like soldiers they scale the wall. They march each on his way; they do not swerve from their paths. They do not jostle one another; each marches in his path; they burst through the weapons and are not halted. They leap upon the city, they run upon the walls, they climb up into the houses, they enter through the windows like a thief.

"The earth quakes before them; the heavens tremble. The sun and the moon are darkened, and the stars withdraw their shining. The LORD utters his voice before his army, for his camp is exceedingly great; he who executes his word is powerful. For the day of the LORD is great and very awesome; who can endure it?" (Joel 2:1-11 ESV).

Your faith is what you make of it. Are you ready for the battle?

"'Yet even now,' declares the LORD, 'return to me with all your heart, with fasting, with weeping, and with mourning; and rend your hearts and not your garments.' Return to the LORD your God, for he is gracious and merciful, slow to anger, and abounding in steadfast love; and he relents over disaster. Who knows whether he will not turn and relent, and leave a blessing behind him, a grain offering and a drink offering for the LORD your God?" (Joel 2:12-14 ESV).

Paul wrote, "I have been crucified with Christ. It is no longer I who live, but Christ who lives in me. And the life I now live in the flesh I live by faith in the Son of God, who loved me and gave himself for me." (Galatians 2:20 ESV). You must be dead to self so you may be strong and steadfast in your actions and in the Spirit of God. If you are not ready, make ready, for the times are soon upon us. I shall give you words of encouragement so you may be prepared for the days ahead.

Go out into the world:

"Proclaim this among the nations: consecrate for war; stir up the mighty men. Let all the men of war draw near; let them come up. Beat your plowshares into swords, and your pruning hooks into spears; let the weak say, 'I am a warrior.' Hasten and come, all you surrounding nations, and gather yourselves there. Bring down your warriors, O LORD. Let the nations stir themselves up and come up to the Valley of Jehoshaphat; for there I will sit to judge all the surrounding nations. Put in the sickle, for the harvest is ripe. Go in, tread, for the winepress is full. The vats overflow, for their evil is great. Multitudes, multitudes, in the valley of decision! For the day of the LORD is near in the valley of decision. The sun and the moon are darkened, and the stars withdraw their shining. The LORD roars from Zion, and utters his voice from Jerusalem, and the heavens and the earth quake. But the LORD is a refuge to his people, a stronghold to the people of Israel" (Joel 3:9-16 ESV).

"Know ye not that the unrighteous shall not inherit the kingdom of God? Be not deceived: neither fornicators, nor idolaters, nor adulterers, nor effeminate, nor abusers of themselves with mankind, nor thieves, nor covetous, nor drunkards, nor revilers, nor extortioners, shall inherit the kingdom of God. And such were some of you: but ye are washed, but ye are sanctified, but ye are justified in the name of the Lord Jesus, and by the Spirit of our God" (1 Corinthians 6:9-11 KJV).

Receive your call for battle with passion and sincerity in your heart. The things of this world are not worth giving up the rewards we shall reap in Heaven. Be steadfast in your works, for a rebellious heart is an inexcusable sacrifice. Brokenness is strong in stature and holy in works, and if you are dead to yourself, as well as the world, you will reap a bountiful harvest of lost souls into the kingdom of God. **"Not because I desire a gift: but I desire fruit that may abound to your account"** (Philippians 4:17 KJV). We can do great things for the Lord in His army if we will come together as holy believers of His glory. Know your part, and seek your mission. Remember: you can do all things through Christ who strengthens you (Philippians 4:13).

The Lord would have you do nothing but remain in His love and strengthen yourselves all that is to come. Are you ready for the battles ahead? If not, pray to God for your mission and let your calling be known. Pray your prayer of faith, and He will answer. The details are unknown, but the battle is certain. Who will overcome and break through to the world's heart, winning souls for the Lord and leaving all they cherish most behind to follow in the Lord's call?

> **"Likewise, ye younger, submit yourselves unto the elder. Yea, all of you be subject one to another, and be clothed with humility: for God resisteth the proud, and giveth grace to the humble. Humble yourselves therefore under the mighty hand of God, that he may exalt you in due time: casting all your cares upon him; for he careth for you. Be sober, be vigilant; because your adversary the devil, as a roaring lion, walketh about, seeking whom he may devour: whom resist steadfast in the faith, knowing that the same afflictions are accomplished in your brethren that are in the world. But the God of all grace,**

who hath called us unto his eternal glory by Christ Jesus, after that ye have suffered a while, make you perfect, establish, strengthen, settle you. To him be glory and dominion for ever and ever. Amen" (1 Peter 5:5-11 KJV).

Who will answer the call?

Call To Repentance

As the skies turn from blue to gray, I look toward the heavens and know one day I will be together with my Father. I see the coming of the times approaching, and I know the body of Christ has yet to come together in unity and holiness but I know that God will bring it to pass. I see people going through motions of praise and worship but my spirit grieves, for the passion has long since departed from the temples. We celebrate emotionalism and worship with extravagant sound systems and fancy lighting, but hearts soon return to wickedness once outside the church doors. Where are the children of God ready to die in response to the call upon their hearts? I search the skies for answers, and I know the Word is the answer to my dilemma.

So many times throughout history, the people and children of God have come together to worship and exalt the Lord on high, but we have failed in our duties to live the worthy example. We all have fallen short of the glory of God. We need to come together and repent. Throughout the history of God's authority over His people, the Lord's children have fallen further away from His love. We seek the hand of God instead of His face. We chase after success and salvation and long for the reputation of being a godly church while denying His power while lacking substance.

The Lord says, "**I have remained, and you have fallen away. I have longed for your love, yet you have given Me none. I have given you all I can give you, yet you remain unsatisfied. Therefore I have given, and I shall also take away. Turn to Me with your whole heart, for you are an unbelieving nation. You say you seek Me, yet I have not seen passion in your eyes. Look for Me, and you will find Me. Search your hearts for Me, and I will be there. Open the door for Me, and I will come in. Let me show you I am your God. I will not force My presence upon you. You must ask, and you shall then receive. You must seek, and you will therefore find. I long to change your hearts and open your eyes to My glory. Yet you must die, and then you shall live. You must sacrifice, and you shall be rewarded. Let Me in, and you will be turned from your iniquities.**"

As the skies turn from gray to black, I know the Lord will be with me, for I have yielded to Him a whole heart and a repentant spirit. "**Let the priests, the ministers of the Lord, weep between the porch and the altar, and let them say, Spare thy people, O Lord, and give not thine heritage to reproach, that the heathen should rule over them: wherefore should they say among the people, Where is their God?**" (Joel 2:17 KJV).

If we as the people of God would unite as one, put aside our differences in beliefs that matter little, and put all prejudice away, we would experience the glory of the Living God of all creation. If we would unite and call upon the Lord, I have no doubt He would show us His face. But we must come to realize the only way to the Lord is at the altar of repentance and total submission to His will.

"**Leave Me at the altar of your heart. Sacrifice your whole heart unto Me, and I will show you wonders. I receive not part, but I will only accept all. For either you will give Me all or give me none. A partial heart is a rebellious one. I am the Lord, and you are the child. Submit your hearts unto Me, and I will spare you from reproach**," says the Lord.

The Lord is holy in all His ways and worthy to be glorified. Do not let your beliefs keep you from the Almighty God. If you are right and yet your neighbor is wrong, does that matter to God? Though your neighbor is right, and you are wrong, does that mean anything to the Father in Heaven? For one is right and one is wrong, but the only way to Heaven is by grace through faith in Jesus Christ. The neighbor cannot therefore be right and you also, except you put aside your differences and unite as one body looking toward Heaven for the Father. Does it matter to God if your neighbor is green and yet you are blue? Is the Lord judgmental towards heritage or race? Did not the Father create all in His own image to the glorifying of His name? Therefore repent, for you have turned from the ways of God. Have you not turned toward the ways of seducing spirits and doctrines of demons?

The Lord speaks to my heart and says, "**One day they will look for Me, and they will not find Me. One day they will search the skies, yet the Lord will have departed from their hearts. One** day they will have hoped, and yet it will be too late. For the Lord is slow to anger and easy to please, yet the Lord says unto you: are you going to keep Me under your wing forever? Have I not given up My life so you might live? Have I not given you all that I am, so that you might live to glorify Me? I show you love and compassion, yet you show Me shame and rebuke My ways. Are you therefore going to be spared in the day of the Lord's judgment? Repent for you are unworthy, and I have shown you great mercy. Lean into Me, and I will give you care. Show Me your passion, and I will give you My favor. Let Me lead you, and you will not fail in your quest. I love you, and you are not worthy, so **repent**," says the Lord.

The Pharisees rebuked the ways of Jesus, the Son of God and the Son of Man, because they thought their traditions and religious beliefs were above reproach. They thought they were right and everyone else was wrong. How long will you continue to go on *knowing* you are right and no one else is? Haven't you suffered yourself long enough?

The Lord says, "**If you will share in your love for Me and extend your care to others, I will show you a greater way.** If you lean into Me, I will show you things you have yet to see. Haven't you seen the Lord? Come to Me, and I will give you life. Repent, and I will show you favor. Let Me live, and I will give you honor. Show Me love, and I will show you glory."

Haven't you gotten tired of being right and everyone else being wrong in their beliefs? Has the world gotten worse, while you have gotten closer to righteousness? Are you above reproach?

The Lord says in Mark 9:35, **"If any man desire to be first, the same shall be last of all, and servant of all."** Have you given up your pride lately to help others? Did not the Pharisees believe they were holy and yet so many others around them unholy? Did not Jesus take the sick and downtrodden in and show them care? Yet you have rebuked them and caused them pain. You have shown them your true heart, for you have not rendered it fully to God. **"Therefore I am against you,"** says the Lord. Have you shown the Lord honor in your actions toward others?

Jesus prayed:

"I do not ask for these only, but also for those who will believe in me through their word, that they may all be one, just as you, Father, are in me, and I in you, that they also may be in us, so that the world may believe that you have sent me. The glory that you have given me I have given to them, that they may be one even as we are one, I in them and you in me, that they may become perfectly one, so that the world may know that you sent me and loved them even as you loved me. Father, I desire that they also, whom you have given me, may be with me where I am, to see my glory that you have given me because you loved me before the foundation of the world. O righteous Father, even though the world does not know you, I know you, and these know that you have sent me. I made known to them your name, and I will continue to make it known, that the love with which you have loved me may be in them, and I in them" (John 17:20-26 ESV).

Has the joy departed from you, and therefore you find yourself burdened to worship and give God praise? You need not be burdened for if you will humble yourselves in the sight of the Lord, He will lift you up (James 4:10). Repent for you have failed in your duties, and ask God to forgive you where you have fallen short. Ask Him to lift you up so you might bring honor and glory to His name. Seek His face, and you will receive His favor.

Nothing should keep you from loving others. Have you forgotten the Lord died not only for you but also for your neighbor in whom you despise? Have you forgotten He loves your neighbor the same as He loves you? Has your pride gotten in the way of loving others? The Lord wants peace not hate. He longs for love and reconciliation not opposition and haughtiness. Have you not despised your neighbor because He believes differently than you? Did not the Son of God die for your neighbor also? Therefore repent for you believe you are right, yet you are wrong, for you cannot hate and also be found favorable in the eyes of the Lord. How long will the body of Christ fight over which part is more valuable?

"For just as the body is one and has many members, and all the members of the body, though many, are one body, so it is with Christ. For in one Spirit we were all baptized into one body—Jews or Greeks, slaves or free—and all were made to drink of one Spirit.

"For the body does not consist of one member but of many. If the foot should say, 'Because I am not a hand, I do not belong to the body,' that would not make it any

less a part of the body. And if the ear should say, 'Because I am not an eye, I do not belong to the body,' that would not make it any less a part of the body. If the whole body were an eye, where would be the sense of hearing? If the whole body were an ear, where would be the sense of smell? But as it is, God arranged the members in the body, each one of them, as he chose. If all were a single member, where would the body be? As it is, there are many parts, yet one body.

"The eye cannot say to the hand, 'I have no need of you,' nor again the head to the feet, 'I have no need of you.' On the contrary, the parts of the body that seem to be weaker are indispensable, and on those parts of the body that we think less honorable we bestow the greater honor, and our unpresentable parts are treated with greater modesty, which our more presentable parts do not require. But God has so composed the body, giving greater honor to the part that lacked it, that there may be no division in the body, but that the members may have the same care for one another. If one member suffers, all suffer together; if one member is honored, all rejoice together.

"Now you are the body of Christ and individually members of it. And God has appointed in the church first apostles, second prophets, third teachers, then miracles, then gifts of healing, helping, administrating, and various kinds of tongues. Are all apostles? Are all prophets? Are

all teachers? Do all work miracles? Do all possess gifts of healing? Do all speak with tongues? Do all interpret? But earnestly desire the higher gifts. And I will show you a still more excellent way" (1 Corinthians 12:12-31 ESV).

Have you set your eyes upon that which you have believed yet not been shown? Are you therefore against something you have not seen yet disregard for your neighbor disregards it also? Does not the Spirit carry with it all gifts? Should you not also seek after that which you have not, yet long to acquire? When will you see the Word is not pick and choose but written for you to live by and direct yourselves in accordance to? Should you not obey every word in the Bible?

Wherefore, how are you against one that heals when the Son of God healed also? How therefore can you despise one that prophecies in His name, and yet there were those that prophesied throughout history? Will not God be the judge of all? You seek to condemn others, yet God will judge you for your lack of faith and indiscretions. Should you not reserve judgment for the Father and Him alone? Pray for your neighbor if he prophecies and it is not by God. For if he repents, he will be spared. Yet, if you repent not, you will be judged accordingly.

Wherefore, how is it you rebuke those who speak mysteries unto God by the spirit, yet you yourself have not? Have you experienced that which you rebuke? Did not the Spirit of God bestow this upon man for His glorifying and the edification of the man's spirit? Therefore how can you call tongues accursed, yet say you love God?

"Therefore I want you to understand that no one speaking in the Spirit of God ever says 'Jesus is accursed!' and no one can say 'Jesus is Lord' except in the Holy Spirit. Now there are varieties of gifts, but the same Spirit; and there are varieties of service, but the same Lord; and there are varieties of activities, but it is the same God who empowers them all in everyone. To each is given the manifestation of the Spirit for the common good. For to one is given through the Spirit the utterance of wisdom, and to another the utterance of knowledge according to the same Spirit, to another faith by the same Spirit, to another gifts of healing by the one Spirit, to another the working of miracles, to another prophecy, to another the ability to distinguish between spirits, to another various kinds of tongues, to another the interpretation of tongues. All these are empowered by one and the same Spirit, who apportions to each one individually as he wills" (1 Corinthians 12:3-11 ESV).

The Bible says that the Spirit divides the gifts to everyone accordingly as He chooses. So, therefore, have you rebuked that which you have not been given?

"Ask, and it shall be given you; seek, and ye shall find; knock, and it shall be opened unto you: for every one that asketh receiveth; and he that seeketh findeth; and to him that knocketh it shall be opened. If ye then, being evil, know how to give good gifts unto your children, how much

more shall your Father which is in heaven give good things to them that ask him?" (Matthew 7:7-8, 11 KJV).

Should not God give you that which you long to have? You have not, because you ask not (James 4:2). God resists the proud, but He gives grace to the humble (James 4:6).

"Submit yourselves therefore to God. Resist the devil, and he will flee from you. Draw nigh to God, and he will draw nigh to you. Cleanse your hands, ye sinners; and purify your hearts, ye double minded. Be afflicted, and mourn, and weep: let your laughter be turned to mourning, and your joy to heaviness. Speak not evil one of another, brethren. He that speaketh evil of his brother and judgeth his brother, speaketh evil of the law, and judgeth the law: but if thou judge the law, thou art not a doer of the law, but a judge. There is one lawgiver, who is able to save and destroy: who art thou that judgest another?" (James 4:7-9, 11-12 KJV).

"**You hypocrites! Have you not seen that I hold Heaven and earth in the palms of My hands? Yet you lack fear as though you control Me. Could I not strike you dead with one glance? I deserve all not part, for I am God, and you are unworthy,**" says the Lord.

Have we power to question the authority of God? Have we any right to say we are worthy of all which has been given? **"Love is a sacrifice. Have you sacrificed unto others that which I have freely given unto you?"** says the Lord. The Lord has given, and

He can take away. The Lord has blessed, and He can condemn. The Lord has yielded unto you fruit, yet He can judge, for the vats are full.

"**Should not repentance be rampant among sinners? You have all sinned yet repent not. Therefore, I shall condemn you unto death for your abominations unto Me,**" says the Lord. Once again, we are all sinners, but not all are rebellious before God. We are all in need of repentance, but the army of God has been called to usher in a new age of repentance before the throne of grace. Those who are living in sin and rampant wantonness of the flesh through the desires of this dark and hate-filled world need guidance to the altar. Shine a light, soldiers, for deliverance only comes by way of rescue.

"**Should not the temple be kept holy? Your heart says yes, yet you have defiled it by evil and corruption. Know you not that your body is a temple of the Holy Spirit which is in you, which you have of God, and you are not your own? Therefore repent for you have defiled the temple of God,**" says the Lord.

Presence brings glory. Sin hinders His glory—yes, even small sin—for sin is sin unto God. Therefore, ask with an open heart for forgiveness, and the Spirit will be made manifest in you.

"**Leave Me at the altar of your heart. If your heart is sacrificed unto Me then your heart and soul are Mine. If Mine, then should you not say and do that which I have instructed you? Therefore repent, because I have made you whole even though you are unworthy,**" says God.

The Lord does not desire judgment but longs for mercy unto all. Yet the Lord shows mercy only to those who seek it. Should not forgiveness only go to those who are passionate for the face of God?

"**Love keeps passion. Passion brings repentance. Therefore, you cannot love Me and still be unrepentant. For either you belong to sin or to Me. I shall not be shared with that which I have cast out of Heaven,**" says the Lord.

Be not deceived: "**All have sinned, and come short of the glory of God,**" (Romans 3: 23 KJV). But those who turn themselves from sinful ways, the same shall be justified in Heaven. "**He that covereth his sins shall not prosper: but whoso confesseth and forsaketh them shall have mercy**" (Proverbs 28:13 KJV). "**Remember therefore from whence thou art fallen, and repent, and do the first works [...] Repent [...] As many as I love, I rebuke and chasten: be zealous therefore and repent**" (Revelation 2:5,16; 3:19 KJV).

Should we not confess our sins unto God so He can forgive us from all iniquity and keep us in His will? "**If we confess our sins, he is faithful and just to forgive us our sins, and to cleanse us from all unrighteousness,**" (I John 1:19 KJV). Let the love you have for others overcome by the light of Christ shining through your weakness, for you are not any more worthy than they. "**Confess your faults one to another, and pray one for another, that ye may be healed. The effectual fervent prayer of a righteous man availeth much**" (James 5:16 KJV). Be redeemed as the Lord's and brought under His wing as children of God.

"Have you still kept that which you long to give? You say, yet your heart is not in it. Therefore, I am displeased. I deserve all not part, for I am God, and you are unholy," says the Lord.

The things we keep from God are those which keep us from forgiveness. Should the Lord forgive those who practice sexual immorality? For if they were heartfelt about repentance, they would turn from their wickedness and pray for strength in not turning back to it. Intentional sin brings forth destruction if repentance is not found. **"Food is meant for the stomach and the stomach for food'—and God will destroy both one and the other. The body is not meant for sexual immorality, but for the Lord, and the Lord for the body"** (1 Corinthians 6:13 KJV).

The Lord is like a farmer. The crops which are raised by His own labor are those yielded unto increase. Yet the weeds intercede some growth, therefore, the Lord weeds out those which need weeding. Should not the Lord only labor for those which long to grow and prosper? Yet if the crop has no desire to grow, the Lord will allow the plant to wither and die, and eventually He will cast the unwanted plant into the fire where unwanted or dead crops are burned. Should the Lord show favor unto crops which are above pruning and reproach? No, but He shall instead remove those which prosper among the weeds and burn the rest.

"Have mercy upon me, O Lord, for I am in trouble: mine eye is consumed with grief, yea, my soul and my belly. For my life is spent with grief, and my years with sighing: my strength faileth because of mine iniquity, and my bones are consumed. I was a reproach among all mine enemies, but especially among my neighbours, and a fear to mine acquaintance: they that did see me without fled from me. I am forgotten as a dead man out of mind: I am like a broken vessel. But I trusted in thee, O Lord; for I have called upon thee: let the wicked be ashamed, and let them be silent in their grave. Let the lying lips be put to silence; which speak grievous things proudly and contemptuously against the righteous.

"Oh how great is thy goodness, which thou hast laid up for them that fear thee; which thou hast wrought for them that trust in thee before the sons of men! Thou shalt hide them in the secret of thy presence from the pride of man: thou shalt keep them secretly in a pavilion from the strife of tongues. Blessed be the Lord: for he hath showed me his marvelous kindness in a strong city. For I said in my haste, I am cut off from before thine eyes: nevertheless thou heardest the voice of my supplications when I cried unto thee. O love the Lord, all ye saints: for the Lord preserveth the faithful, and plentifully rewardeth the proud doer. Be of good courage, and he shall strengthen your heart, all ye that hope in the Lord," (Psalms 31:9-12, 14-24 KJV).

Worthy Of the Battle

As the days progress with increasing intensity and new battles, wonders in the heavens are opened up to signal signs of the coming Lord and Savior Jesus Christ. The times are shown throughout world events, and the world is calling out to Him. However, these words are dead and unheard—void and separated from the will of God. For the will of God is at hand, and He will have the way of the Father. The strength is increasing, and the call shall soon be heard, but the dreariness of the dark sky and Satan's angels are manifesting more each day. The glory of God has yet to manifest in the promised way of His prophecies, but the sounds of His coming are heard upon the growing winds.

As the winds pick up in the distance, I see the signs of the coming future, and I look for the evidence of His coming. What shall be the signs of Your coming and of the end of the world, oh God?

Jesus answers:

> "Being asked by the Pharisees when the kingdom of God would come, he answered them, 'The kingdom of God is not coming in ways that can be observed, nor will they say, "Look, here it is!" or "There!" for behold, the kingdom of God is in the midst of you.' And he said to the disciples, 'The days are coming when you will desire to see one of the days of the Son of Man, and you will not see it. And they will say to you, "Look, there!" or "Look, here!" Do not go out or follow them. For as the lightning flashes and lights up the sky from one side to the other, so will the Son of Man be in his day. But first he must suffer many things and be rejected by this generation.

"'Just as it was in the days of Noah, so will it be in the days of the Son of Man. They were eating and drinking and marrying and being given in marriage, until the day when Noah entered the ark, and the flood came and destroyed them all. Likewise, just as it was in the days of Lot—they were eating and drinking, buying and selling, planting and building, but on the day when Lot went out from Sodom, fire and sulfur rained from heaven and destroyed them all—so will it be on the day when the Son of Man is revealed. On that day, let the one who is on the housetop, with his goods in the house, not come down to take them away, and likewise let the one who is in the field not turn back.

"'Remember Lot's wife. Whoever seeks to preserve his life will lose it, but whoever loses his life will keep it. I tell you, in that night there will be two in one bed. One will be taken and the other left. There will be two women grinding together. One will be taken and the other left.' And they said to him, 'Where, Lord?' He said to them, 'Where the corpse is, there the vultures will gather'" (Luke 17:20-37 ESV).

One night, I asked the Lord, "Why did you make the galaxy and all of the planets and stars if you only created us?" He answered quickly, "**I made them for those of you who seem to know yet have no idea. I gave you mysteries to witness throughout time so that I may be glorified in the end. I shall be glorified in the end.**" The Lord made me realize He put the galaxies here for us to wonder and amaze at all the universe. And yet we wonder and study the created when we could be intimately searching and knowing the Creator.

Why do you let us go on like this Lord? For one day we shall be gathered together in Your name, and the world will have known the power of God. How long shall the world last until the end, oh God?

He answers through Peter:

> "Knowing this first of all, that scoffers will come in the last days with scoffing, following their own sinful desires. They will say, 'Where is the promise of his coming? For ever since the fathers fell asleep, all things are continuing as they were from the beginning of creation.' For they deliberately overlook this fact, that the heavens existed long ago, and the earth was formed out of water and through water by the word of God, and that by means of these the world that then existed was deluged with water and perished. But by the same word the heavens and earth that now exist are stored up for fire, being kept until the Day of Judgment and destruction of the ungodly.
>
> "But do not overlook this one fact, beloved, that with the Lord one day is as a thousand years, and a thousand years as one day. The Lord is not slow to fulfill his promise as some count slowness, but is patient toward you, not wishing that any should perish, but that all should reach repentance. But the day of the Lord will

come like a thief, and then the heavens will pass away with a roar, and the heavenly bodies will be burned up and dissolved, and the earth and the works that are done on it will be exposed.

"Since all these things are thus to be dissolved, what sort of people ought you to be in lives of holiness and godliness, waiting for and hastening the coming of the day of God, because of which the heavens will be set on fire and dissolved, and the heavenly bodies will melt as they burn! But according to his promise we are waiting for new heavens and a new earth in which righteousness dwells. Therefore, beloved, since you are waiting for these, be diligent to be found by him without spot or blemish, and at peace." (2 Peter 3:3-14 ESV)

The Lord doesn't want anyone to be deceived about the time of His coming. I urge you to seek truth in your quest to know God intimately. Don't let others teach you their indoctrinated beliefs, but always stand and lean into the Lord's understanding. **"Trust in the Lord with all thine heart and lean not unto thine own understanding. In all thy ways acknowledge him, and he shall direct thy paths. Be not wise in thine own eyes: fear the Lord, and depart from evil,"** (Proverbs 3:5-7 KJV).

Is the world ready for battle, oh God? The coming of these times are upon us, yet the warriors have not been mounted. The Lord is drawing all His soldiers together for battle, but so many in the world want to wait until Sunday morning. All other times are off the clock. They long for the lunch hour to roll around so the words of God's coming judgment will diminish and dissipate from their thoughts.

How long, oh God, will you let this go on? I seek truth and understanding, yet I long for more than just these. I want Your all, oh Lord. Will You judge Your own? Has the world mercy from You, oh God?

The Lord answers through Peter in saying:

"The Lord knoweth how to deliver the godly out of temptations, and to reserve the unjust unto the day of judgment to be punished: but chiefly them that walk after the flesh in the lust of uncleanness, and despise government. Presumptuous are they, self-willed, they are not afraid to speak evil of dignities. Having eyes full of adultery, and that cannot cease from sin; beguiling unstable souls: an heart they have exercised with covetous practices; cursed children.

"These are wells without water, clouds that are carried with a tempest; to whom the mist of darkness is reserved for ever. For when they speak great swelling words of vanity, they allure through the lusts of the flesh, through much wantonness, those that were clean escaped from them who live in error. While they promise them liberty, they themselves are the servants of corruption: for of whom a man is overcome, of the same is he brought in bondage.

"For if after they have escaped the pollutions of the world through the knowledge of the Lord and Saviour

Jesus Christ, they are again entangled therein, and overcome, the latter end is worse with them than the beginning. For it had been better for them not to have known the way of righteousness, than after they have known it, to turn from the holy commandment delivered unto them. But it is happened unto them according to the true proverb, the dog is turned to his own vomit again; and the sow that was washed to her wallowing in the mire" (2 Peter 2:9-10; 14;17-22 KJV).

Although many of you may be angry at these words, I would only have you know the truth. I know the ways and traditions of man, but who says the traditions are correct? Draw near to God, and He will draw near to you. God is truth. Seek God, and you will find the knowledge you have longed to acquire.

The winds are increasing, and the days are growing shorter. How long are you going to naively chase after that which you have not seen or felt, but why not chase after the Almighty God whom you can both see and feel? How you ask? The Lord renders wonders through us all. We should see God in each other for His kingdom dwells in each of us. We should be open to the Holy Spirit's manifestations, for the will of God is that everyone be saved and delivered. The Holy Spirit is not a quiet little breeze. Be not deceived. The manifestation of the Spirit of God only comes to the willing. You must be open to the moving of His presence within or you are going to be left with nothing but wisps and trails of glamour. The Word teaches us, **"Quench not the Spirit"** (1 Thessalonians 5:19 KJV). **"Moreover the word of** the Lord came to me, saying, Son of man, eat thy bread with quaking, and drink thy water with trembling and with carefulness" (Ezekiel 12:17-18 KJV).

We should be careful, now more than ever, for the times are drawing closer, and the manifestation of our God shall soon be seen. Be not deceived—the manifestation of His Spirit will be even greater than that of the early Church.

Ezekiel speaks of the coming time in saying:

"Then he brought me back to the door of the temple, and behold, water was issuing from below the threshold of the temple toward the east (for the temple faced east). The water was flowing down from below the south end of the threshold of the temple, south of the altar. Then he brought me out by way of the north gate and led me around on the outside to the outer gate that faces toward the east; and behold, the water was trickling out on the south side.

"Going on eastward with a measuring line in his hand, the man measured a thousand cubits, and then led me through the water, and it was ankle-deep. Again he measured a thousand, and led me through the water, and it was knee-deep. Again he measured a thousand, and led me through the water, and it was waist-deep. Again he measured a thousand, and it was a river that I could not pass through, for the water had risen. It was deep enough to swim in, a river that could not be passed through. And he said to me, 'Son of man, have you seen this?'

"Then he led me back to the bank of the river. As I went back, I saw on the bank of the river very many trees on the one side and on the other. And he said to me, 'This water flows toward the eastern region and goes down into the Arabah, and enters the sea; when the water flows into the sea, the water will become fresh. And wherever the river goes, every living creature that swarms will live, and there will be very many fish. For this water goes there, that the waters of the sea may become fresh; so everything will live where the river goes. Fishermen will stand beside the sea.

"From Engedi to Eneglaim it will be a place for the spreading of nets. Its fish will be of very many kinds, like the fish of the Great Sea. But its swamps and marshes will not become fresh; they are to be left for salt. And on the banks, on both sides of the river, there will grow all kinds of trees for food. Their leaves will not wither, nor their fruit fail, but they will bear fresh fruit every month, because the water for them flows from the sanctuary. Their fruit will be for food, and their leaves for healing'" (Ezekiel 47:1-12 ESV).

The Lord will pour out His Spirit in such intensity the world will know He is here. The power of God's Spirit will come in such force the seas will be healed. The deadened world will open up and be cleansed from the sin and corruption. The Lord will release a great outpouring on earth, and we are a part of it! But be not deceived—the soldiers and faithful children shall be left and protected. The rest shall be thrown into the midst of confusion. To him who overcomes, he shall receive heavenly rewards from the Most High God. Holy of Holy and Righteous King, is the Lord.

Isaiah wrote:

> "And though the Lord give you the bread of adversity and the water of affliction, yet your Teacher will not hide himself anymore, but your eyes shall see your Teacher. And your ears shall hear a word behind you, saying, 'This is the way, walk in it,' when you turn to the right or when you turn to the left.
>
> "And he will give rain for the seed with which you sow the ground, and bread, the produce of the ground, which will be rich and plenteous. In that day your livestock will graze in large pastures, and the oxen and the donkeys that work the ground will eat seasoned fodder, which has been winnowed with shovel and fork. And on every lofty mountain and every high hill there will be brooks running with water, in the day of the great slaughter, when the towers fall. Moreover, the light of the moon will be as the light of the sun, and the light of the sun will be sevenfold, as the light of seven days, in the day when the LORD binds up the brokenness of his people, and heals the wounds inflicted by his blow" (Isaiah 30:20-21; 23-26 ESV).

The Lord will bind up the breach of his people, turn them from their lying divinations, and ultimately, He will execute judgment on the wicked. The Lord says to my heart, "**Though the people know Me, they know Me not with their hearts but with their cares, for their cares are in the world, and yet they seek Me to help them live in the world.**"

How long, oh God, until You bind the breach of Your people? I seek Your face and Your tender mercies. I am called for battle; therefore, I stand with utmost boldness and work toward the victory I will one day claim in the name of Jesus:

"O LORD, do not your eyes look for truth? You have struck them down, but they felt no anguish; you have consumed them, but they refused to take correction. They have made their faces harder than rock; they have refused to repent. Then I said, 'These are only the poor; they have no sense; for they do not know the way of the LORD, the justice of their God. I will go to the great and will speak to them, for they know the way of the LORD, the justice of their God.' But they all alike had broken the yoke; they had burst the bonds.

"Therefore a lion from the forest shall strike them down; a wolf from the desert shall devastate them. A leopard is watching their cities; everyone who goes out of them shall be torn in pieces, because their transgressions are many, their apostasies are great. 'How can I pardon you? Your children have forsaken me and have sworn by those who are no gods. When I fed them to the full, they committed adultery and trooped to the houses of whores. They were well-fed, lusty stallions, each neighing for his

neighbor's wife. Shall I not punish them for these things?' declares the LORD; 'and shall I not avenge myself on a nation such as this? Go up through her vine rows and destroy, but make not a full end; strip away her branches, for they are not the LORD's'" (Jeremiah 5:3-10 ESV).

Now while most of these passages speak to Israel about their spiritual adulteries committed against God, how true are these same words to the Church today? We have committed spiritual adultery against Him and given ourselves over to the world. Only a remnant now remains, and it is time for this remnant to rise up from the ashes and unite as one body in spirit and in truth—to grow in prayer and supplication before the Lord while mounting our forces against the darkness of this world. Now is the time!

God grows weary of the unfaithful. One day the Lord will deal justice to those who have taken His love for granted and lived in the ways of the world for their own desires. The Lord will bind up the breach of His people and send them through the cleansing fountains of His promise. But next will come adversity. The Lord would have you be faithful unto death. How many would give their lives for the Almighty God? For the Lord came to earth to die for you so you might live. For whosoever seeks to save His life in that time shall lose it, but whosoever seeks to lose His life for Christ's sake shall find eternal life (Mark 8:35).

And [Jesus] said, Whereunto shall we liken the kingdom of God? or with what comparison shall we compare it? It is like a grain of mustard seed, which, when it is sown in the earth, is

less than all the seeds that be in the earth: but when it is sown, it groweth up, and becometh greater than all herbs, and shooteth out great branches; so that the fowls of the air may lodge under the shadow of it** (Mark 4:30-32 KJV).

Let the seed of the kingdom of God manifest in you, growing daily so our Father in Heaven may work through you in glorifying His Son.

All things do I give you so you may prosper abundantly, and so you may know the days are upon us. Let the light shine into the growing darkness. Rise up soldiers of the cross, for the battle is near. Fight for the Lord and His kingdom. The Lord shouts to you for victory in His name. Speak truth into the dreary gloom of night, and let the light of God Almighty shine through you.

Fellow warriors, the days are nigh when the darkness shall come against you swiftly. Start preparing for battle for the war has already begun. Train to excel in the Lord, and lead your fellow soldiers into battle with your heads high and your eyes upon the heavens. Keep the Lord in your sights, and you shall emerge victorious and with life eternal. Your life is in the Lord's hands. Let Him guide you into glory. God be with you all.

Victory In Our Lord Jesus

As the times turn from darkness to light, I know the Almighty God bestows upon us victory in the name of Christ Jesus our Lord and Savior. For we have triumphed over evil. We have sealed the bondages of sin and death and cast them into

Hell with the churning of time's torment. As our eyes are filled with the glory bestowed from God Almighty, we emerge into eternal fellowship with the Holiest of Holy, the Author and Finisher of our Faith.

The Lord has claimed you and adopted you as His own. He has placed His name upon you and set you free from the bondages of sin and death. He has granted you authority over the darkness and the ability to set the captives free (Luke 4:18). For where those who live after the flesh fail, those who walk in the Spirit overcome.

> "**For the law of the Spirit of life has set you free in Christ Jesus from the law of sin and death. For God has done what the law, weakened by the flesh, could not do. By sending his own Son in the likeness of sinful flesh and for sin, he condemned sin in the flesh, in order that the righteous requirement of the law might be fulfilled in us, who walk not according to the flesh but according to the Spirit. For those who live according to the flesh set their minds on the things of the flesh, but those who live according to the Spirit set their minds on the things of the Spirit. For to set the mind on the flesh is death, but to set the mind on the Spirit is life and peace. For the mind that is set on the flesh is hostile to God, for it does not submit to God's law; indeed, it cannot. Those who are in the flesh cannot please God.**
>
> "**You, however, are not in the flesh but in the Spirit, if in fact the Spirit of God dwells in you. Anyone**

who does not have the Spirit of Christ does not belong to him. But if Christ is in you, although the body is dead because of sin, the Spirit is life because of righteousness. If the Spirit of him who raised Jesus from the dead dwells in you, he who raised Christ Jesus from the dead will also give life to your mortal bodies through his Spirit who dwells in you"** (Romans 8:2-11 ESV).

When God Almighty saved you, He freed you from the bondages of sin and death, giving you liberty and freedom to live in the Spirit of God. You should declare victory in the name of Jesus, for you are free from the authority of Satan. He only has the power you give him. **"So when the Son sets you free, you shall be free indeed"** (John 8:36 KJV). Jesus gives you authority over all things. He places no limits on what you can do for Him. Set your eyes upon the heavens and declare with faith that you have set your limits as high as the stars of the sky sitting in reverence of the Almighty.

Be not deceived. Where Satan fails, you can overcome by the power and glory of Jesus Christ. Where his boundaries are, you shall proceed with glory. For while the devil has authority over the flesh, you live not of the flesh but in the Spirit. So, therefore, by the grace of God, you are free from the bonds and strongholds placed upon you by Satan. For where the flesh is weak, the Spirit is strong and willing. Be not deceived, it says in Romans 8:8 (KJV), **"So then they that are in the flesh cannot please God."** Read it again. You have been set free from the bondages of sin and called to crucify the flesh (Galatians 5:24).

So the victory has been given to you by the grace of God for the glorification of His name.

He has sealed His love inside you to manifest and give you all things in accordance to His will. For surely God is love, and no one can say God is love but by the Spirit. Also no one can say Jesus is Lord but by the Spirit (1 Corinthians 12:3). So when you are free from the bondages of sin and death, you are reborn to live in accordance to His divine will. Therefore cause all sin cease to reign and dwell in your mortal bodies. Allow the love of God to manifest and flow throughout your soul so your actions might glorify His wonderful name.

When Satan was given authority over mortal flesh, He became ruler of this earth. The only power Satan possesses has been granted to him, but God has given him dominion over the flesh of the earth to do with the world as he pleases to a large extent. But as we are not of the flesh, be not confined to the flesh but walk forth in the Spirit of God. You live in a much more prosperous and free kingdom. Those of the flesh will die, for the flesh is surely finite. But the Spirit is infinite and carries all believers filled with His presence into eternal life with our Christ Jesus.

We must be dead to the flesh and live in accordance to the Spirit, manifesting those things in our lives which are of purity and holiness. We are not held captive by the sinful nature of the world but instead have been set free. We live under the authority of the Lord and now have authority over sin and Satan. Demons tremble at the name of Jesus. I've seen it and declare its truth.

As written in the book of James, **"the devils also believe, and tremble"** (James 2:19 ESV). Therefore do not forsake your inheritance to live in the flesh and darkness of this world, but live after that which is greater and take within your grasp the grace of God and the promise of eternal life.

Mount up the soldiers of God for battle. Surely Satan's army cannot withstand that of the Spirit's. **"For God's camp is very great: for he is strong that executeth his word"** (Joel 2:11b KJV). Not only are we free from the bondages of sin and death, but we are given power over the darkness of this world. The power of God bestows great authority, and none is greater than the Lord's. **"For as many as are led by the Spirit of God, they are the sons of God. For ye have not received the spirit of bondage again to fear: but ye have received the Spirit of adoption, whereby we cry Abba, Father. The Spirit itself beareth witness with our spirit, that we are the children of God: and if children, then heirs of God, and joint-heirs with Christ; if so be that we suffer with him, that we may be also glorified together"** (Romans 8:14-17 KJV).

We shall face adversity and persecution. We shall face trials and tribulations. We shall face temptations and the valley of shadow and of death. Let not your heart be troubled, for we should all count it worthy to suffer in the name of our Lord Jesus. We should rejoice in persecution and glorify God in the Highest. **"For I reckon that the sufferings of this present time are not worthy to be compared with the glory which shall be revealed in us. And we know that all things work together for** good to them that love God, to them who are the called according to his purpose" (Romans 8:18, 28 KJV).

For God sent his only begotten Son to earth to die for us that we all might be counted worthy by the shedding of His blood. Sent in the form of sinful flesh and yet without, by the Spirit of God condemning sin in the flesh, the Son died on the cross so that we might be healed and made whole in the name of Christ Jesus our Lord. So thereby I count it worthy to suffer for the name of our Lord Jesus for I have claimed victory in His name, setting me free from the bondages of sin, and by the Spirit of God cleansing me from all iniquity.

So therefore child of God if one lives after the flesh, one is under the authority of the flesh and thus under the hand and rule of Satan. But let not your heart be troubled, but live after that of the Spirit, claiming the victory so you may live in eternal fellowship with the Lord. Surely these things shall be established within you for they are of God. The Spirit of God gives to all to profit withal. We know not where the Spirit of God always leads, but we seek after the Spirit so these things may be accomplished in the Lord Jesus. **"Likewise the Spirit helps us in our weakness. For we do not know what to pray for as we ought, but the Spirit himself intercedes for us with groanings too deep for words. And he who searches hearts knows what is the mind of the Spirit, because the Spirit intercedes for the saints according to the will of God"** (Romans 8:26-27 ESV).

The victory is yours to claim. So claim it and be free from sin's grasp. For we that are of the Spirit are strong while those of the flesh are weak and overcome. For while the flesh is weak, the spirit is willing (Matthew 26:41). Do not let the darkness dictate your life, but follow after the Spirit. Rebuke the flesh and live holy, consecrated, and sanctified lives in the name of Jesus Christ, glorifying Him in all deeds, counting it worthy to suffer in His name. For you are established by the power and authority of the Spirit of God to live and overcome worldly flesh.

Live not in the world, but live for God and Him alone. Let your path be directed by the Almighty. Let His Word be a lamp unto your feet and a light for your path (Psalm 119:105). Holy is His name, and He is worthy of all praise, honor, and glory. Surely as the stars shine high above, the Lion of the tribe of Judah overcomes and holds within His grasp full authority over Satan. Let God's will be done in your life and declare the victory in His name tonight to live holy for the glorification of His name.

I depart from you, being not worthy but under the servitude of the Almighty God. I live to please Him, so I will face the world with a bold face. I live as a dweller in the world but not of the world, for I live under the kingship of Jesus Christ (John 9:5; John 17:16). Though the world turns towards sin and corruption, I am not moved. My feet are planted upon the solid rock of Christ. I declare the victory and reserve to Him the honor and glory. The storm is blowing in, growing stronger each night, dwelling within the confines of the flesh. But it penetrates not that of the Spirit, neither can it overcome the peace God Almighty has given us within. For where the world shall fall short, we will live on and overcome.

The world faces darkness and death. It faces judgment and wrath. We live in a world of bitter mistrust, evil, and deceit. It is worthy of the punishment of death in the highest degree. "But none of these things move me, neither count I my life dear unto myself, so that I might finish my course with joy, and the ministry which I have received of the Lord Jesus, to testify the gospel of the grace of God" (1 Corinthians 20:24 KJV). For I have claimed victory in the name of Jesus Christ, our Lord. Let His name be manifested and glorified forever. Amen.

Sounding the Battle Cry

"'Yet even now,' declares the LORD, 'return to me with all your heart, with fasting, with weeping, and with mourning; and rend your hearts and not your garments.' Return to the LORD your God, for he is gracious and merciful, slow to anger, and abounding in steadfast love; and he relents over disaster. Who knows whether he will not turn and relent, and leave a blessing behind him, a grain offering and a drink offering for the LORD your God?

"Blow the trumpet in Zion; consecrate a fast; call a solemn assembly; gather the people. Consecrate the congregation; assemble the elders; gather the children, even nursing infants. Let the bridegroom leave his room, and the bride her chamber. Between the vestibule and the altar let the priests, the ministers of the LORD, weep and say, 'Spare your people, O LORD, and make not your heritage a reproach, a byword among the nations. Why should they say among the peoples, "Where is their God?"'

"Then the LORD became jealous for his land and had pity on his people. The LORD answered and said to his people, 'Behold, I am sending to you grain, wine, and oil, and you will be satisfied; and I will no more make you a reproach among the nations.

"'I will remove the northerner far from you, and drive him into a parched and desolate land, his vanguard into the eastern sea, and his rear guard into the western sea; the stench and foul smell of him will rise, for he has done great things.

"'Fear not, O land; be glad and rejoice, for the LORD has done great things! Fear not, you beasts of the field, for the pastures of the wilderness are green; the tree bears its fruit; the fig tree and vine give their full yield.

"'Be glad, O children of Zion, and rejoice in the LORD your God, for he has given the early rain for your vindication; he has poured down for you abundant rain, the early and the latter rain, as before.

"'The threshing floors shall be full of grain; the vats shall overflow with wine and oil. I will restore to you the years that the swarming locust has eaten, the hopper, the destroyer, and the cutter, my great army, which I sent among you'" (Joel 2:12-25 ESV).

"'And it shall come to pass afterward, that I will pour out my spirit upon all flesh; and your sons and your daughters shall prophecy, you old men shall dream dreams, your young men shall see visions: and also upon the servants and upon the handmaids in those days will I pour out my spirit.

"'Also, proclaim ye this among the Gentiles; prepare war, wake up the mighty men, let all the men of war draw near; let them come up: beat your plowshares into swords, and your pruning hooks into spears: let the weak say I am strong. Assemble yourselves, and come, all ye heathen, and gather yourselves round about: thither cause thy mighty ones to come down, O Lord'" (Joel 2:28-29; 3:9, 11 KJV).

"'Son of man, speak to your people and say to them, If I bring the sword upon a land, and the people of the land take a man from among them, and make him their watchman, and if he sees the sword coming upon the land and blows the trumpet and warns the people, then if anyone who hears the sound of the trumpet does not take warning, and the sword comes and takes him away, his blood shall be upon his own head. He heard the sound of the trumpet and did not take warning; his blood shall be upon himself. But if he had taken warning, he would have saved his life. But if the watchman sees the sword coming and does not blow the trumpet, so that the people are not warned, and the sword comes and takes any one of them, that person is taken away in his iniquity, but his blood I will require at the watchman's hand.

"'So you, son of man, I have made a watchman for the house of Israel. Whenever you hear a word from my mouth, you shall give them warning from me. If I say to the wicked, O wicked one, you shall surely die, and you do not speak to warn the wicked to turn from his way, that wicked person shall die in his iniquity, but his blood I will require at your hand. But if you warn the wicked to turn from his way, and he does not turn from his way, that person shall die in his iniquity, but you will have delivered your soul.

"'And you, son of man, say to the house of Israel, thus have you said: "Surely our transgressions and our sins are upon us, and we rot away because of them. How then can we live?" Say to them, "As I live," declares the Lord GOD, "I have no pleasure in the death of the wicked, but that the wicked turn from his way and live; turn back, turn back from your evil ways, for why will you die, O house of Israel?"'" (Ezekiel 33:2-11 ESV).

Have you felt that stirring somewhere amidst your heart and collarbone? Or that stirring in your spirit that rises up to a swell before pummeling the back of your spine? There is something to the manner in which the Spirit of God has begun to move among His people. There is no more time for delay and spiritual absenteeism. We must be there for the march toward lurking evil. Too many souls are paying the price of early death and eternal torment. Where are the preachers of repentance in the world today? Blessings and prosperity only last until the wells run dry, but God's Spirit brings spiritual prosperity in overflowing abundance. Gather your weapons, and get in line. We need the victory—if it's only for one soul, the battle will have been worth it.

Sound the battle cry. Raise the crimson flag of Jesus Christ. Let the voice of your commands for righteousness and repentance be heard. Let His mighty warriors be called up to holy war against the evil forces which have spread throughout the earth. His light will keep you through the adversity ahead, so leap into action with the fellow warriors in your company. Intercede for others. Pray for the lost and aimless. Cry out to the heavens, and lay yourselves upon the altar of God giving Him every single piece of your mind, body, and soul. Allow His Spirit to envelop you in His protection.

Now RISE UP! Be prepared. Be diligent. Sound the alarm for others and bring them into His love and care. Give them to God, and He will give them peace and their missions for the journey ahead. The days will be long, and the nights will be dark, but the morning shall see eternal souls arisen into everlasting peace in God's presence. He shall manifest His Spirit and bring glory and honor to His name through the selfless sacrifice of those who have responded in obedience. If you will repent and turn from your ways, He will keep you during the dangerous times ahead.

Lift each other up. Seek the One True God who gives all to those who believe in His name. Get ready, oh army not desired. The world may not want you, but the Lord mounts you up with the wings of eagles (Isaiah 40:31). Place your hope in the Lord so you can run and not grow weary in the days ahead and amid your special operations for the Lord. Be ready for the war of the ages. The spiritual storm is upon us, but you are ready and prepared. You have gained all to give all. You have laid your life upon the altar of brokenness and repentance to perform the duties of our Almighty God. You have responded faithfully to the call, so now therefore ask God to fulfill His promises for the days ahead:

> **"Ask rain from the LORD in the season of the spring rain, from the LORD who makes the storm clouds, and he will give them showers of rain, to everyone the vegetation in the field. For the household gods utter nonsense, and the diviners see lies; they tell false dreams and give empty consolation. Therefore the people wander like sheep; they are afflicted for lack of a shepherd.**
>
> **"My anger is hot against the shepherds, and I will punish the leaders; for the LORD of hosts cares for his flock, the house of Judah, and will make them like his majestic steed in battle"** (Zechariah 10:1-3 ESV).
>
> **"Return to your stronghold, O prisoners of hope; today I declare that I will restore to you double"** (Zechariah 9:12 ESV).

Turn to the Lord your God so you can become the mighty warrior that God is raising you up to become. Demand truth from the false prophets in the church who see lies and utter ungodly promises of material prosperity and worldly gain by way of divining spirits and false gods. They are empty consolations not worthy of the kingdom of God. Do not allow the people of God to wander aimlessly with despair in their hearts and no direction because the shepherds are found lacking.

If we, as mighty warriors of the Lord, will come together as His own, not being separated by race, gender, or heritage, we can overcome the barriers and strongholds Satan has put before us. We will march on our ways, and we will not break our ranks for the Lord God is with us.

Be not deceived. The times are too short to look back. Remember Lot's wife. Look not at what has been but look at what is now ahead. Let your sinful ways be cast aside with your worldly cares so we, as a mighty assembly of warriors and worshipers, can turn the world back to the one true Living God. Let your heart's cry for revival be heard. Let the war begin with you making the decision to make a difference in this life and to fight for the Lord. Join with your fellow warriors by seeking the Lord with every single ounce inside of you. ***Every single ounce of you.***

The Lord speaks against the sinners saying:

"'You only have I known of all the families of the earth; therefore I will punish you for all your iniquities.' Do two walk together, unless they have agreed to meet? Does a lion roar in the forest, when he has no prey? Does a young lion cry out from his den, if he has taken nothing? Does a bird fall in a snare on the earth, when there is no trap for it? Does a snare spring up from the ground, when

it has taken nothing? Is a trumpet blown in a city, and the people are not afraid? Does disaster come to a city, unless the LORD has done it?

"'For the Lord GOD does nothing without revealing his secret to his servants the prophets. The lion has roared; who will not fear? The Lord GOD has spoken; who can but prophesy?'" (Amos 3:2-8 ESV).

"'I will strike the winter house along with the summer house, and the houses of ivory shall perish, and the great houses shall come to an end,' declares the LORD" (Amos 3:15 ESV).

Unless we as a people of God unite and repent for the abominations our nation has committed against the Lord God, we will be judged accordingly. God is merciful beyond measure, but the abominations of wickedness have overflowed the vats of judgment, and He will soon measure them for the iniquities which have been committed. God has forbidden anyone with wickedness and rebellion in their hearts to inherit eternal life, so repent before it's too late. Join the army of the Lord and see His power manifested throughout the world. Be a part of the call! The times are upon us for the great move of the Lord, but if united in "liberty and justice for all," we can't find a way to get Jesus back into our lives and our country, He will judge us accordingly.

"Woe to you, scribes and Pharisees, hypocrites! For you clean the outside of the cup and the plate, but inside they are full of greed and self-indulgence. You blind

Pharisee! First clean the inside of the cup and the plate, that the outside also may be clean.

"Woe to you, scribes and Pharisees, hypocrites! For you are like whitewashed tombs, which outwardly appear beautiful, but within are full of dead people's bones and all uncleanness. So you also outwardly appear righteous to others, but within you are full of hypocrisy and lawlessness.

"Woe to you, scribes and Pharisees, hypocrites! For you build the tombs of the prophets and decorate the monuments of the righteous, saying, 'If we had lived in the days of our fathers, we would not have taken part with them in shedding the blood of the prophets.' Thus you witness against yourselves that you are sons of those who murdered the prophets. Fill up, then, the measure of your fathers. You serpents, you brood of vipers, how are you to escape being sentenced to hell?

"Therefore I send you prophets and wise men and scribes, some of whom you will kill and crucify, and some you will flog in your synagogues and persecute from town to town, so that on you may come all the righteous blood shed on earth, from the blood of righteous Abel to the blood of Zechariah the son of Barachiah, whom you murdered between the sanctuary and the altar. Truly, I say to you, all these things will come upon this generation" (Matthew 23:25-36 ESV).

Aren't you tired of going to church on Sunday mornings expecting God to do something, but all you get are small wafts of the holy smell of His divine bread? Aren't you tired of the passionless worship?

"Passion is the key to presence. If you seek Me, have passion for Me, so that I might be passionate in My giving to you," says the Lord.

Do you think worship is going to the building down the street with His name on the sign and sitting through a service while pondering the lunch menu possibilities? You are the temple! The building is the place of worship. You can go into the building, but you are the temple and are called to keep it holy. **"What? Know ye not that your body is a temple of the Holy Ghost which is in you, which ye have of God, and ye are not your own?"** (1 Corinthians 6:19). The church is the body of believers.

Where have our beliefs and values gone? We have conformed to pleasing the eyes and scratching the itching ears of a covetous and idolatrous nation. The opinions and demands of the world and their religious schedules are as the Pharisees were in the days when Christ walked upon the earth as a man. God knows your heart. Quit going through the motions and get passionate for Him so you do not face the judgment ahead.

Jesus spoke to the churches saying:

"I know your works: you are neither cold nor hot. Would that you were either cold or hot! So, because you are lukewarm, and neither hot nor cold, I will spit you out of my mouth. For you say, I am rich, I have prospered, and I

need nothing, not realizing that you are wretched, pitiable, poor, blind, and naked. I counsel you to buy from me gold refined by fire, so that you may be rich, and white garments so that you may clothe yourself and the shame of your nakedness may not be seen, and salve to anoint your eyes, so that you may see. Those whom I love, I reprove and discipline, so be zealous and repent. Behold, I stand at the door and knock. If anyone hears my voice and opens the door, I will come in to him and eat with him, and he with me. The one who conquers, I will grant him to sit with me on my throne, as I also conquered and sat down with my Father on his throne. He who has an ear, let him hear what the Spirit says to the churches" (Revelation 3:15-22 ESV).

Sound the cry for battle so you can lead your wayward brothers and sisters back to the true path. Let the war against the movement of Hell and Satan's forces be manifested throughout the world so we might prevail against the evil sweeping across our world. Let's take back by force what our ancestors have freely given up. Let's transform this world back into a godly, trusting nation by breaking down strongholds in the name of Jesus Christ and through faith in the movement of His Holy Spirit. Lead the troops into battle with the sound and cry of victory in the name of Jesus.

"Behold, the name of the LORD comes from afar, burning with his anger, and in thick rising smoke; his lips are full of fury, and his tongue is like a devouring fire; his breath is like an overflowing stream that reaches up to the neck; to sift the nations with the sieve of destruction, and to place on the jaws of the peoples a bridle that leads astray.

"You shall have a song as in the night when a holy feast is kept, and gladness of heart, as when one sets out to the sound of the flute to go to the mountain of the LORD, to the Rock of Israel. And the LORD will cause his majestic voice to be heard and the descending blow of his arm to be seen, in furious anger and a flame of devouring fire, with a cloudburst and storm and hailstones" (Isaiah 30:27-30 ESV).

Repent and be spared the coming judgment from the Lord on this nation which has turned its back. Turn once again to the ways of the Lord, for his mercy ceases for those who refuse to turn from their abominations. The Lord declares once again, **"If my people, which are called by my name, shall humble themselves, and pray, and seek my face, and turn from their wicked ways; then will I hear from heaven, and will forgive their sin, and will heal their land"** (2 Chronicles 7:14 KJV).

He said He would heal our lands only if we humble ourselves, pray, and then seek His face. He promised the Israelites, and the same promises holds true for us, that if these few steps are completed then forgiveness and healing would come. The great outpouring of God will come by repentance, prayer, and the breaking down of strongholds by engaging the enemy in close combat through regular and intense spiritual warfare.

Have you been so foolish to think God is someone to call upon only in late hours of distress? God requires your undivided attention and commitment. Why have you given Him the scraps from the table when you, yourself, are not worthy to be in the house? Repent or judgment will come upon you.

I don't care how many times you have prayed the sinner's prayer, how long you have been a member of a church, or how faithful you are in attendance. If you do not have a relationship with Jesus Christ, you are doomed to be judged as the rebellious sinner you are. If you pray to my Holy God only when you need something or the vats of material prosperity run low, you do not know Him. I am not judging you but giving you the hard facts from the Word of the Lord.

Repent, join the army of God, and go into battle at the sound of the trumpet of war. The storm is upon us, and you have been fast asleep.

Wake up! Wake up, oh nation not desired, and see the coming of times upon you! Look to the skies and see the storm approaching and the war already begun.

"The wilderness and the dry land shall be glad; the desert shall rejoice and blossom like the crocus; it shall blossom abundantly and rejoice with joy and singing. The glory of Lebanon shall be given to it, the majesty of Carmel and Sharon. They shall see the glory of the LORD, the majesty of our God.

"Strengthen the weak hands, and make firm the feeble knees. Say to those who have an anxious heart, 'Be strong; fear not! Behold, your God will come with vengeance, with the recompense of God. He will come and save you.'

"Then the eyes of the blind shall be opened, and the ears of the deaf unstopped; then shall the lame man leap like a deer, and the tongue of the mute sing for joy. For waters break forth in the wilderness, and streams in the desert; the burning sand shall become a pool, and the thirsty ground springs of water; in the haunt of jackals, where they lie down, the grass shall become reeds and rushes.

"And a highway shall be there, and it shall be called the Way of Holiness; the unclean shall not pass over it. It shall belong to those who walk on the way; even if they are fools, they shall not go astray. No lion shall be there, nor shall any ravenous beast come up on it; they shall not be found there, but the redeemed shall walk there. And the ransomed of the LORD shall return and come to Zion with singing; everlasting joy shall be upon their heads; they shall obtain gladness and joy, and sorrow and sighing shall flee away" (Isaiah 35 ESV).

"As the whirlwind passes, so is the wicked no more: but the righteous is an everlasting foundation" (Proverbs 10:25 KJV).

"Oh sing to the LORD a new song, for he has done marvelous things! His right hand and his holy arm have worked salvation for him. The LORD has made known his salvation; he has revealed his righteousness in the sight of the nations. He has remembered his steadfast love and faithfulness to the house of Israel. All the ends of the earth have seen the salvation of our God.

"Make a joyful noise to the LORD, all the earth; break forth into joyous song and sing praises! Sing praises to the LORD with the lyre, with the lyre and the sound of melody! With trumpets and the sound of the horn make a joyful noise before the King, the LORD!

"Let the sea roar, and all that fills it; the world and those who dwell in it! Let the rivers clap their hands; let the hills sing for joy together before the LORD, for he comes to judge the earth. He will judge the world with righteousness and the peoples with equity" (Psalm 98 ESV).

The Lord promises that His army will earn great victories for Him, and we will be bound together by His name. He will give us strength to destroy wickedness, bind demons, and even perform healing and miracles in His name. Believe the words of the Lord when He says, **"Truly, truly, I say to you, whoever believes in me will also do the works that I do; and greater works than these will he do, because I am going to the Father. Whatever you ask in my name, this I will do, that the Father may be glorified in the Son. If you ask me anything in my name, I will do it" (John 14:12-14 ESV).

Believe in the power of His name, and you will do wonders the world has never seen before by the power of the Holy Spirit who is in you. Leave the world of complacency and fight the battle to win the victory which is sure to be won. The stars shine the glory of God and his power. His mercy endures forever. Amen.

Surely, we will overcome the world and live eternally with our Father and Creator. Holy is His name on Earth and in Heaven. Jesus has given you His Word, thereby giving Himself, so we might find healing and strength in times of affliction and persecution. The world will hate you, but you are not of this world just as He was not of the world (John 17:14). So go forth, and shine light into the dark places, and win souls for the Lord God, our Savior.

The Guiding Hope of Glorious Destiny

The sun shines over a moonless gaze of the translucent glory of the wondrous works of the Father. I dwell in the emeralds of the voyaging sea of passion, and I long for the hope of those helpless to call upon the name of my Lord God. I see the passion in the eyes, but yet there is nothing to free them from their bondage. I chase after the invisible, leaving trails of the past behind me upon the waters—like a star on a million year journey of providing light to the eye of one special soul.

I see the revelation of the coming sun upon the moonlight in the darkness of the despairing children. I gaze upon all which has come to be, and yet there is no one for the job ahead. I gasp in amazement at the approaching battle-arrayed warriors, and in complete awe of the mercies of such a profound God, I pray for the perseverance to lead more from the depths of darkness in these desperate moments. Only trust and hope can get us through these few final hours of existence before the coming of the Lord.

Oh how I do wonder at the coming of the morning which glows in the awesome shining of a magnificent and fixed return of our eternal King. Glory and majesty bestowed, supreme wonder marches boldly into a night air otherwise mired in ever-increasing moments of tragedy. Oh how I must stay at the foot of God's throne in supplication and remembrance of the blessed hope which all may come to know and understand.

Remarkable shining of a new age of dawning light sinks upon the eternal state of humankind which has never known the wonders of our amazing Father in such abundance. Oh shall I see it in the days to come! Unworthy and unable to muster anything but fear and trepidation, I stand in awe of the power of the One who has set time to come to a standstill for the glory of Heaven to come to earth. Oh how the stars shine in such remarkable ways of wonder.

Has the sunshine in the rain ever left you standing cold? Has the eternal promise ever been abandoned? Has the Father's love ever rendered you void deep inside the heart of passion for the Son? God forbid. The holy, divine guiding light upon a terrestrial path of meekness and humble solitude takes me forth as potential prey among the wolves—but I am ready to fight! Oh how will my purpose with God ever fit into the never-ending puzzle of the battle plan?

The Lord says we have been left untouched as the anointed of His own hand's discipline. Will I be made whole as a treasure among treasures? Refined as gold and pure as the unblemished Lamb are the sacrificial warriors of the called. Has the blood covered all? Has the blameless been kept under the wing of the Most High? I will keep His name upon my heart in trembling and adoration. Oh how precious is the name of the Son of the Most High God. Holy Father and the Living Word, you are most revered! Loved and cherished above all, oh how my love runs deep for Him!

Glowing in the gentle night breeze with the storm on the horizon, this voyage is not my own but under the servitude of someone far beyond comprehension or comparison. Oh how He is feared among all, for His secret He has shown to those who love and obey Him. The star will never fade. The line will never end its continuous voyage of time in existing infinite eternity. Has the diamond been fashioned by any other hand than that of the Creator's? His reign will never cease. He lives, for His love is a guiding light for the hope I grip tightly in the presence of a promised and glorious future.

The world will fade. The sun reluctantly dies, and the moon soon falls from the hanging eternal balance of time and space. The grass will wither, and the flowers will fall (Isaiah 40:7; 1 Peter 1:24; James 1:11). Satan will be overwhelmingly overcome and beaten as an unwanted mongrel, and I will cherish the victory by eternally reigning with the Father and the Son of my glorious destiny. The shadow shall not be moved, and the line will not surpass the birth of its existence. As well, I shall not be moved. I will not be left or forgotten. I will live. I will reign in royalty as the son of the Most High. I will overcome and surpass all who oppose. I will shine on as a light of the Son in whom I most love.

The sweetest flower I have ever smelled, it grows as the desirous longing of eternal wonder and love, never-ending and shining light and hope like the stars above. I will not die but live on. The Lion will overcome, and all will fall and praise the name of the Nazarene whom I have yearned to see. His love runs with overflowing abundance—like a river without burden—but manifests as a seed of hope. Give glory to the Lamb of God—He is worthy to be praised!

Final Words

As I sail on in the path of an amazing adventure, the treasures and rewards ahead lead me into these vicious battles with courage and strength. The Lord is my Rock. I shall not be moved. As the winds blow into the midst of my voyage with the Almighty Lamb of God, I face them with boldness and authority.

Though I am expected to overcome all obstacles I face, I know the storm will rise against this vessel, the sails will catch wind and ride the waves of the sea, and all of those opposing forces will manifest and wage war against me.

But I have liberty in Christ, and I will help lead the army of God into victory, for the skies show the glory of the coming Lord. All will be reconciled, and the Living God will show power in Heaven as well as on Earth. The journey will be hard fought, but in the end I shall prevail. I will live for the purpose of my glorious destiny, guided by the hope of the Lord Jesus Christ, and aided by the magnifying power of His Holy Spirit.

As I drift forward into the never-ending flow of time, I see the strength along the horizon looming closer as the days wear on. I will one day be within its reach. But for the moment I must persevere. I must face the harsh weather, the evil opposition, the trials and hardships, and the oppressive forces of darkness. I will love my neighbor as myself as I give abundantly, seeking nothing in return. The reflections of past waves dance across the ocean's natural canvas, and I stand in awe of the glory of the Lord.

I have gained all to give all, for whosoever seeks to be first shall certainly be last (Matthew 20:16). My cross have I taken up with joy, and I have sacrificed all for the journey. The war will be tough. The battles will be harsh and pain inflicting. But my faith is in the heavens. I see Jesus in the throne room of God, high and lifted up. I see the rain of the seed of increase flowing abundantly upon the earth. I see the fire of the glory of God manifesting in His people while the enemy is vanquished in heaps and ashes. The undulated glory of God rises and flows forth, and I hear the sound of a trumpet in the distance. It is the sound of battle. Intense conflict, manifesting love, and overwhelming power have reached the bow of my vessel amidst visions and promises of the future.

"From the end of the earth will I cry unto thee, when my heart is overwhelmed, lead me to the rock that is higher than I; for thou hast been a shelter for me, and a strong tower from the enemy. I will abide in thy tabernacle forever: I will trust in the covert of thy wings. Selah. In God is my salvation and my glory: the rock of my strength, and my refuge is in God. Trust in him at all times; ye people, pour out your heart before him: God is a refuge for us. Selah" (Psalms 61:2-4; 62:7-8 KJV).

Pour out your hearts to the Living God, and give Him every single drop of your being. Blood, sweat, and tears shall be left upon the altar of God *today*. Give all to win the war. Let the voyage be a victorious and joyful one. I will sing praises to the Lord until the end of time. His name rings in my ear giving me songs of gladness all the day long. **"The Lord is on my side; I will not fear: what can man do unto me?** (Psalms 118:6 KJV).

As the waves pass by in an eternal drift of time, I see souls of the great harvest gathered together to give praise to the eternal King. A beautiful moon shines so bright and full of life as the waters caress the bow of my holy vessel. The dawn of time in a new light approaches, and I yearn to see the Lord.

Therefore, I will carry on as an unworthy servant of God, having been recruited into His army as a soldier, living as a leader of the faith, and giving praise to the Creator of my soul.

He shall guide me into victory, and I will dwell in the house of my God forever and ever. Amen.

The Lion Will Overcome!
(A Prophecy of Judgment on America)

The country that once knew God; the country that God has given power over all, and the country that has raised its name so that all might know its might: the Lord has given, and the Lord shall take it away.

More dominant than all, its power great and its wickedness greater, the Lord gives, and the Lord takes away. The once faithful, obeying, and true nation has turned in the same way that Israel turned away. He has given all that is true, and He shall take it away, so that you may know the Lord your God is Almighty and still ruler of all the Earth.

Proclaim a fast. Humble yourselves before the Lord so that you may be spared from this evil tragedy coming against you. **"Oh evil and treacherous country, in the way that Nineveh was abolished so shall you be in that great and terrible day that the Lord judges,"** says God Almighty.

The Lion shall overcome. Half shall be given, and half shall He take away. Your dominance will be given to another, and your brother in whom you most trust shall turn against you.

Fear the Lord and His judgment, for His wrath will be carried out among you. The Lord has given, and half shall He take away. Turn from your treacherous ways, oh evil and unbelieving country. Your death shall be as the death of Assyria. The Lord has given, and so in the same manner shall He take away.

Turn, oh evil country, from your abominations, and seek the one true God who deals all things to those who believe.

The Lord Almighty has spoken, and He shall therefore carry out His promise to those who do not turn from wickedness.

The Lord has given, and the Lord also takes away, so in the things that are therein told, be true to these for surely as the stars shall shine the Lion will overcome.

Made in the USA
Coppell, TX
27 May 2020